Bennett on CONSUMER BANKRUPTCY:
A Practical Guide for Canadians

Bennett on
CONSUMER
BANKRUPTCY:
A Practical Guide
for Canadians

Frank Bennett

Self-Counsel Press
(a division of)
International Self-Counsel Press Ltd.
Canada   USA

Self-Counsel Press acknowledges the financial support of the Government of Canada through the Canada Book Fund (CBF) for our publishing activities.

Printed in Canada.

First edition: 2014

Library and Archives Canada Cataloguing in Publication

Bennett, Frank, 1942-, author

    Bennett on consumer bankruptcy : a practical guide for Canadians / Frank Bennett.

(Self-Counsel legal series)

Includes index.

Issued in print and electronic formats.

ISBN 978-1-77040-189-1 (pbk.).--ISBN 978-1-77040-940-8 (epub).--ISBN 978-1-77040-941-5 (kindle)

    1. Bankruptcy--Canada--Popular works. I. Title. II. Series: Self-Counsel legal series

KE1499.2.B45 2013	346.7107'8	C2013-908012-0
KF1524.85.B45 2013		C2013-908013-9

Self-Counsel Press
(a division of)
International Self-Counsel Press Ltd.

North Vancouver, BC	Bellingham, WA
Canada	USA

CONTENTS

15 COMMON QUESTIONS

GLOSSARY

APPENDIX I: EXCERPTS FROM THE *BANKRUPTCY AND INSOLVENCY ACT*

APPENDIX 2: ADDITIONAL READING AND CONTACT INFORMATION

APPENDIX 3: SUPERINTENDENT'S STANDARDS

THE DOWNLOAD KIT

INDEX

FIGURES

SAMPLES

NOTICE TO READERS

Laws are constantly changing. Every effort is made to keep this publication as current as possible. However, the author, the publisher, and the vendor of this book make no representations or warranties regarding the outcome or the use to which the information in this book is put and are not assuming any liability for any claims, losses, or damages arising out of the use of this book. The reader should not rely on the author or the publisher of this book for any professional advice. Please be sure that you have the most recent edition.

PREFACE

I wrote a companion book for the small- and medium-sized business debtor called *Bennett's A–Z Guide to Bankruptcy: A Professional's Handbook* published by CCH Canadian Limited in Toronto. That book is similar to this one dealing with the same topics except from a business perspective. This book is devoted entirely to consumer and small-business debtors who want to take advantage of the favourable rules for consumers. It explains the bankruptcy process and alternatives available to the consumer debtor.

Canadian bankruptcy laws continue to change. For the first-time consumer debtor, bankruptcy is an easy solution to overwhelming debt problems. For individuals who wish to repeat bankruptcy proceedings, there are more restrictions, although not severe, when using the bankruptcy system.

According to the statistics kept by the Office of the Superintendent of Bankruptcy, in the year 2001, 92,836 Canadian consumers took bankruptcy protection. There were 79,453 consumer bankruptcies and 13,383 consumer proposals. Parliament has enacted laws which encourage consumers to make deals, or proposals as they are called, to the creditors rather than go fully bankrupt. With a declining economy, and with events following September 11, 2001, there were likely to be increases in consumer insolvencies. We live in an inflated economy, and at any given time, consumers cannot pay their credit card accounts and mortgage payments even with much lower interest rates. The recession of 2008 is continuing. In the year 2012, 118,398 consumers took bankruptcy protection. Of this number, 71,495 filed for bankruptcy and 46,903 filed consumer proposals.

People incur financial difficulties for many different reasons including marital strife or divorce, loss of job or plant closure, over-extension on credit cards, death of a key person in a business, and the bankruptcy of their businesses. Our bankruptcy laws are not onerous; in fact, they encourage individuals and companies to take protection from creditors who are pressing collection of their accounts. Being bankrupt does not have serious consequences for most individuals. Being bankrupt does not even mean that the debtor loses all his or her assets. In fact, with good legal advice, some assets can be protected against creditors. It's important to see a lawyer first if you are considering filing for bankruptcy. Sometimes, certain assets can be protected; sometimes, the lawyer may advise you not to take protection.

Parliament changed the main bankruptcy laws somewhat in 1992, again in 1997, and then again in 2009 to encourage consumers and small-business debtors to make proposals to creditors rather than go bankrupt. The mechanical procedures for both proposals and bankruptcy were streamlined. Bankruptcy is no doubt the popular remedy. It is still very easy for a person to go bankrupt and it is still very easy for an individual to get discharged without too much difficulty or hardship. The system does not penalize the honest but unfortunate debtor, but it does free the debtor from most of his or her debts. However, there are few advantages for consumers to make proposals.

In this book, I give basic information to consumer and small-business debtors about the bankruptcy system. Lawyers, accountants, and financial planners and counsellors may find the book a good primer to Canada's bankruptcy laws. In an office setting, I would take the individual consumer debtor through one or two interviews before recommending whether first, the client is a candidate for protection, and second, if so, how to go about it. I always ask the client for three pieces of paper: first, a list of assets; second, a list of debts or liabilities; and lastly, a list of questions. These lists focus the client on the problem at hand. With this information, I can give legal advice about the effects of bankruptcy on each of the assets and liabilities, as well as give answers to all the questions posed. Sometimes, the consumer debtor does not want to go into bankruptcy, and in these cases, some form of proposal or restructuring with the creditors may be possible.

It sounds easy. For most people, bankruptcy is a quick and easy solution to debt problems.

For the most part, individuals —

- want to know when they can get their credit cards back;

- want to know when it's over; and

- do not care about the forms and formality, they just want to get credit again.

I hope that I take the mystique out the bankruptcy process and that more people will better understand how the system can work for them.

In preparation of this edition, I wish to thank Irving Burton, Jordan Rumanek, and Karen Adler, experienced trustees in bankruptcy in Toronto for their thoughtful comments and suggestions. I also wish to thank Eileen Velthuis, my critical editor who asked many skill-testing questions in her review of the book.

Frank Bennett
Toronto

Chapter I
WHAT IS BANKRUPTCY?

This book offers a review of the bankruptcy process for individuals, primarily consumer debtors, who are in financial difficulty. This book does not review the bankruptcy process for small-business corporations. (Corporations cannot be consumers, but small-business persons may be able to take advantage of consumer bankruptcies and proposals; more on that later.) For readers who are interested in small corporate bankruptcies, see *Bennett's A–Z Guide to Bankruptcy: A Professional's Handbook* published by CCH Canadian Limited in Toronto.

In this chapter, the individual who may be facing bankruptcy can review the general outline of the bankruptcy process. It raises questions, the answers with which the consumer should consider before going into bankruptcy. Subsequent chapters expand each of the specific areas, and more. While bankruptcy is considered a last resort remedy for financial woes, the individual should first consider all remedies in dealing with debt including re-financing assets such as residential homes and condominiums; obtaining credit counselling; entering into some form of consolidation plan or order to pay something over time; making of a consumer proposal under the *Bankruptcy and Insolvency Act* to his or her creditors; or some other informal arrangement with his or her creditors. As a result of amendments to bankruptcy legislation over the last 20 years, these options can be more viable than going straight into bankruptcy.

Bankruptcy is for individuals who have significant debt. An individual shouldn't necessarily consider bankruptcy for amounts under $100,000. First-time bankrupts get a "get out of jail free card" right away. Over a lifetime, they will not get the same concession if they file again. Repeat bankruptcy is on the rise with consumers and for individuals who may have some assets of value and for individuals who are self-employed, it is best to see a lawyer first before seeing a trustee in bankruptcy. While all lawyers have professional training and must be licensed by the Law Societies across Canada to practise, the individual should seek counsel from a lawyer who has experience in the bankruptcy and insolvency field. The initial or subsequent visit to review the individual's financial affairs may lead one not to file for bankruptcy at all, but rather to negotiate some other settlement. In addition, the individual may have a valuable asset that may be lost in a bankruptcy. As will be discussed, the trustee in bankruptcy works for both the debtor and the creditors. The trustee is also an officer of the court and responsible to the court and to the Office of the Superintendent of Bankruptcy, the licensing body for trustees. Therefore, it is very difficult for a trustee to advise a debtor not to proceed with some form of insolvency protection when the individual is experiencing financial difficulties.

1. Defining Bankruptcy

Bankruptcy is a legal process which an individual debtor can take to protect himself or herself from creditors who are taking legal action to collect their accounts and debts.

Creditors may send letters and call the individual on a regular basis to pay the account, or more likely, creditors employ collection agencies who consistently call the individual. Ultimately, the creditor commences a lawsuit to collect, and if the individual does not have an adequate defence, the creditor obtains judgment. This judgment can be enforced easily through garnishment proceedings against the individual's employer. This may finally force the debtor into bankruptcy.

Taking bankruptcy protection protects the individual debtor from further collection tactics. Bankruptcy involves a transfer of most of the debtor's assets to a licensed trustee who sells them and distributes the monies amongst the debtor's creditors. The debtor, however, can keep some exempt assets such as RRSPs. A debtor may be an individual person, a partnership, or a corporation. Bankruptcy wipes out, or releases most of the debts to creditors when the bankrupt obtains his or her discharge and allows the bankrupt to start all over again. The honest but unfortunate bankrupt person is generally entitled to a fresh start.

The bankruptcy process is governed by the *Bankruptcy and Insolvency Act* which is a federal statute. This statute was first enacted in Canada in 1919 and has been amended several times. The Act is the same throughout Canada and applies equally in Newfoundland and Labrador as it applies in British Columbia or in any of the territories.

The effect of taking bankruptcy proceedings is like waving a magic wand over the debtor's creditors as it makes most legal proceedings to collect debts disappear. Taking bankruptcy protection relieves an individual debtor of his or her debts and provides instant relief and protection from creditors, collection agencies, and their lawyers who are suing the debtor. Taking bankruptcy protection stops collectors from collection agencies telephoning, faxing, emailing, and harassing the debtor. Taking bankruptcy protection stops employers from deducting monies from the debtor's salary for the benefit of seizing creditors. For both the individual and the corporation, once bankruptcy happens, it feels as if a dark cloud over the debtor has lifted and disappeared.

After an individual goes into bankruptcy, creditors are generally prevented from taking legal actions against the debtor or against the debtor's property. By operation of law, creditors are prevented from taking lawsuits, seizures, garnishments against the debtor's wages, distress and similar related proceedings against the debtor without special permission of the court. The *Bankruptcy and Insolvency Act* provides an honest debtor with relief against overbearing creditors and affords the debtor with a second, and in some cases a third, chance to establish himself or herself.

Once a debtor takes bankruptcy protection, the process under the law also allows for the orderly and fair distribution of a bankrupt person's non-exempt assets amongst all the debtor's creditors according to a scheme of priority. Exempt assets are assets that the individual can keep if he or she files for bankruptcy. They would include, for example, tools of trade and household furnishings up to certain amounts, and registered retirement savings funds. Non-exempt assets for individuals are assets that are over and above certain thresholds. For example, the individual will be able to keep registered retirement savings funds except for monies invested within one year before bankruptcy. More about exemptions in section **6.** and in Chapter 6.

The *Bankruptcy and Insolvency Act* sets out a priority scheme so that there is seldom any argument about the distribution of monies once the assets are sold. The provisions under the Act prevent creditors from scrambling to seize assets. It allows a debtor who is overburdened with debt, but has some assets, to transfer them to a trustee who will then sell and distribute the proceeds in a fair and equitable manner. This transfer of title to the assets happens automatically when the debtor takes protection. In practice, the consumer debtor rarely has any assets of value except for his or her salary. As a result, there is seldom any distribution of dividends to creditors. In short, bankruptcy allows the honest debtor to start all over again without the burden of debt.

2. Read This Book First!

Many people who go through the bankruptcy process do not need to consult a lawyer. Their affairs are neither technical nor complicated. These types of debtors are generally employees who lost their jobs through plant closures, business bankruptcies, receivership, or for other causes, and they are now unable to service the monthly debt to credit card holders such as VISA, MasterCard, and American Express, and to pay the mortgages on their homes.

However, if there are more serious financial problems which the debtor can identify from the list in section **3.**, and the debtor falls within one or more of them, then it is advisable to see a lawyer first. Once the debtor files for bankruptcy, the debtor is technically in bankruptcy and except in the rarest of cases, the debtor will not be able to reverse the process. If the debtor has any doubts about going into bankruptcy, again the debtor should *see a lawyer first*. The debtor should not sign any bankruptcy papers unless the debtor is satisfied of the consequences and is prepared to deal with them once in bankruptcy.

After seeing a lawyer, the debtor may have other remedies available to resolve the financial difficulties at which time the debtor may elect not to file for bankruptcy. This decision as to whether to file for bankruptcy is critical as once the debtor files for bankruptcy protection, the date becomes a focal point for many objectives under the Act. These are discussed throughout the book.

Lawyers are generally not able to list themselves in the telephone directory or advertise to the public by specialty or expertise unless they are certified as such experts by their provincial or territorial law society. Therefore, if the debtor has serious financial problems, it is necessary to go to a general practitioner in law or an accountant and if that professional cannot answer the questions, the debtor should request a referral to a bankruptcy and insolvency lawyer. Alternatively, the debtor may call the Law Society or the Canadian Bar Association and they may be able to suggest a number of lawyers who practise in this area. It is very important to deal with a lawyer who specializes in this area, as these types of lawyers have special knowledge and skill and they will save the debtor time and expense and usually give advice more quickly. However, if the debtor consults a general practitioner, he or she will have to review the law in the area and advise the debtor on questions. This may be time consuming and may be as or more expensive even though the general practitioner may come out with the same answers and give the same advice as the specialist.

In short, if there are no valuable assets, the debtor is likely a consumer debtor and will not require the services of a lawyer. However, if the debtor has substantial debt, has many valuable assets, or is a high wage earner or is self-employed, the debtor should see a lawyer first before filing for bankruptcy.

At this stage, the debtor should sit down and review this book and prepare questions to ask the lawyer if the debtor chooses to see one first, or questions to the trustee if the debtor goes directly to a trustee's office. In either case, the debtor should clearly understand the process before making an assignment into bankruptcy.

3. Learning about Bankruptcy before It Happens

Almost every consumer debtor who is having financial difficulty and is not paying bills on time knows that he or she is in financial difficulty and is headed for bankruptcy unless there is a sudden influx of money. Debtors do not have to be mathematicians to know they can't pay their bills. Once consumer debtors realize that they have more money going out of their bank account monthly than coming into their bank account, that they are no longer paying their bills in ordinary course, they may realize they are probably headed for bankruptcy. Usually, paying off one credit card with another is a typical signal of financial sickness. It's just a matter of time until the credit card companies catch up on their collections and drive the individual to see a trustee in bankruptcy.

Consumer debtors who can't pay their debts now, and consumer debtors who know they won't be able to pay them in the near future, need financial assistance.

There are two well-known tests for bankruptcy. First, there is the cash-flow test; that is, whether the debtor is generally unable to pay the bills as they come in. Most suppliers of credit give their customers some time to pay the bills. Usually it is about 30 days from the time the supplier sends the bill. Give or take a few days either way, the debtor has about 20 days to pay the bill in full. If the debtor does not pay the bill, virtually all suppliers charge interest on overdue accounts which can range from 12 percent to more than 40 percent per annum. Take Bell Canada, for example: At the time of writing this book, if an individual does not pay on time, Bell Canada charges 42.58 percent per annum! With interest rates that high, it is easy to see how one can face financial instability quickly.

The second test to determine whether the consumer debtor is headed for bankruptcy is called an asset test; namely, the debtor would not have sufficient assets if all his or her assets are sold at a fairly conducted sale under legal process to pay the debts.

Let me give three examples of the asset test. First, everyone knows that when you drive a new car off the lot, the value of the car depreciates significantly in excess of 20 percent minutes later.

Likewise, with jewellery which is often marked up 300 to 500 percent of its wholesale value: It's one thing to buy an engagement ring at a jewellery store for $1,000 plus tax and it's another thing to pawn it for a few hundred dollars months later.

Last, there is no value in used clothing. While a new suit may have cost more than $1,000, it has virtually no value on resale. So, when adding up a debtor's assets, the debtor must be fully aware that his or her assets will fetch a very low dollar.

Most consumer debtors who are unable to pay their bills tend to be thoroughly optimistic that their problems will go away or that tomorrow will be different and that things will change. Unfortunately, almost all of these consumer debtors are wrong. Tomorrow comes and goes and the problems surrounding the debtors continue to increase to the point where the debtors want to be put out of their misery. This rarely happens to the personal debtor as the creditor usually stands back and attempts to collect from the debtor by some lawful means. Consumer creditors seldom force the consumer debtor into bankruptcy. Instead, they assign their accounts to a collection agency which is paid a commission on collections. Collectors are notorious for harassing people, suing in Small Claims Court, and then garnisheeing or attaching the debtor's wages. Collectors do not earn a living by putting consumers into bankruptcy. Their job is to squeeze the consumer into paying something every month under the threat of seizure and/or threat of bankruptcy.

Sometimes, a consumer debtor is lucky. A creditor will put the debtor into bankruptcy. But this costs money and creditors are very reluctant to "spend good money after bad" (meaning there is little or no chance of recovery). A creditor will force a consumer debtor into bankruptcy if the creditor believes that the debtor has stashed away money or other assets, or if the debtor has recently gifted some property, such as a summer cottage or RRSP, to a spouse, partner, or children. Most other times, the consumer debtor has to take the steps to go bankrupt; that is, file for voluntary bankruptcy, or technically, file an assignment in bankruptcy as the pressure becomes impossible to bear.

How does the individual consumer know that he or she is insolvent or soon to be bankrupt under the bankruptcy system? There are many early warning signs, each of which may not be the final straw that forces the issue, but added up, the signs generally point to a course of direction which is virtually irreversible: bankruptcy.

Early warning signs for consumers include:

- ◆ Loss of a job.

- ◆ Marital or partnership separation.

- ◆ Over-extension of credit cards.

- ◆ Use of one credit card to pay the other ("robbing Peter to pay Paul").

- Running out of money just after payday.

- Unanticipated large expenditures.

- Failing to pay the credit card balances in full each month.

- Harassment by several creditors or collection agencies.

- Impulse buying for merchandise that is really unnecessary, and using credit cards for payment.

- Garnishment of wages.

- Gambling or substance addiction.

If the consumer is having difficulty in making ends meet on a regular basis, then he or she will qualify to go bankrupt. Unless the consumer takes proceedings authorized by the Act, the consumer is not technically bankrupt: The individual is insolvent. Insolvency means the person is unable to pay his or her debts in the ordinary course. All bankrupts are insolvent persons, but not all insolvent persons are bankrupt. An insolvent person can continue to work, be employed, or carry on business until creditor harassment becomes intolerable. Then the debtor may take protection under the *Bankruptcy and Insolvency Act*. Bankruptcy generally lasts for a minimum of nine months, and in serious cases where creditors object to the bankrupt's discharge, for several years, and in some cases, the bankrupt never gets discharged. See Chapter 3 for the time sequence involved in bankruptcy.

The following are ways that a consumer can go bankrupt under the *Bankruptcy and Insolvency Act*.

First, the consumer can make an "assignment." An Assignment is the document that transfers or conveys all of the consumer's assets to a person called a trustee in bankruptcy. This trustee in bankruptcy is licensed by the federal government in Ottawa, namely the Department of Industry, pursuant to the *Bankruptcy and Insolvency Act*. The trustee in bankruptcy administers the consumer's affairs by collecting and selling all the assets and ultimately paying the proceeds to creditors under a prescribed formula. More about the trustee in bankruptcy and distribution later.

The assignment is a voluntary act by the consumer debtor; that is, the debtor does it by himself or herself without going to the courts. Much of this book is devoted to assignments by debtors.

The second way a person can go bankrupt under the Act is by being put into bankruptcy by one or several creditors. If this happens, it is called an involuntary bankruptcy. The creditor issues a legal proceeding called "an application for a bankruptcy order."An application is like a statement of claim issued by a creditor in the Superior Courts in each of the provinces and territories to collect a debt, except in the case of an application, the creditor is suing on its own behalf and on behalf of all creditors. In fact, it is really a class action of all creditors against the consumer debtor.

The application alleges that the debtor owes a sum of money, that the debt has not been paid, that there are other creditors who are also owed money, and that for the benefit of all creditors, the consumer debtor should be placed into bankruptcy. The consumer debtor has the right to defend the application, and after a short period of time, there is a trial to determine whether the consumer debtor should be placed into bankruptcy. If the application is successful, the court then makes what is called a "bankruptcy order"against the consumer debtor; in other words, the court issues an order that simply places the consumer debtor into bankruptcy.

This remedy is used by creditors who do not get paid and who take the legal steps to put the debtor into bankruptcy. The process is adversarial; that is, there is a legal dispute which is heard before a judge. After the hearing, the judge decides one way or another. This hearing or trial can be costly for both sides if the consumer debtor can and wants to defend on good grounds. Creditors do not generally force consumer debtors into bankruptcy as there are rarely substantial assets to administer and the expense of doing so would be borne by the application creditor. However, a consumer debtor will rarely defend the application for a bankruptcy unless the consumer debtor is concerned about some asset or assets that may have questionable exemptions.

Last, a consumer debtor may consider making a deal or settling with his or her creditors. Governed by the *Bankruptcy and Insolvency Act*, this process is called a "proposal."A proposal is a contract or an agreement by a consumer debtor and the creditors to pay something less, as a general rule, than the full amount that is owing to the creditors. There are many rules under the Act that apply to consumer proposals.

Here is an example of a consumer proposal: The consumer debtor may offer (and the creditors may choose to accept) 40 cents on every dollar that is owed. If the consumer debtor owes $100,000 to all his or her ordinary creditors, the debtor may propose to pay $40,000 with the result that the debtor will be relieved or discharged from paying the balance of $60,000. If the creditors vote against the terms of the proposal or say "no,"then the consumer debtor is not automatically put into bankruptcy. If the creditors vote "yes"or in favour of the proposal, the consumer debtor will not be put into bankruptcy, but the debtor is bound by the terms of the agreement. In these cases, the creditors will accept the good intention and good faith of the consumer debtor to make a deal, thereby the consumer debtor avoids bankruptcy and going through the bankruptcy process from meetings to discharge.

Over the last 20 years, the federal government has amended the *Bankruptcy and Insolvency Act* several times to permit a consumer debtor to take advantage of the provisions relating to consumer proposals. Division II of Part III of the Act specifically deals with consumer proposals. The consumer proposal is discussed later in this book, and particularly, in Chapter 10. It is the recommended solution if the consumer debtor has gainful employment. Creditors will receive something rather than nothing in a bankruptcy; the consumer debtor then is not bankrupt.

3.1 Qualifying for bankruptcy

The consumer debtor must meet certain conditions under the *Bankruptcy and Insolvency Act* in order to go bankrupt:

♦ The consumer debtor must owe at least $1,000 to any of his or her creditors.

♦ The consumer debtor must commit "an act of bankruptcy."

While there are many acts of bankruptcy, the usual one connected to consumers is that the consumer must be unable to meet the regular bill payments to creditors according to their terms. For example, if the debtor does not pay his or her bills within 30 days as promised, then the debtor is unable to pay those debts in the ordinary course; or the debtor must not have enough property which, if sold at a fair market sale, would be sufficient to pay all the creditors in full. For instance, if the debtor were to list all his or her personal possessions and then have a liquidator value them, the likelihood is that their total value would be very low compared to the size of the debt.

If the consumer debtor meets these two conditions, the consumer debtor is considered insolvent. The consumer debtor then qualifies to go bankrupt voluntarily or he or she can be put into bankruptcy by any one of the creditors if the creditors are willing to go to court to do it.

3.2 Alternatives to bankruptcy

While the consumer debtor may qualify under the criteria above, he or she may wish to avoid bankruptcy if it is possible. Many debtors do not want to go bankrupt as they consider bankruptcy to be irresponsible and a failure financially.

They may also consider their reputation in the community and the stigma attached to bankruptcy, although that factor seems to be diminishing over the last 30 years.

Last, but not least, debtors want to protect their credit rating. Once in bankruptcy, it may take years to re-establish credit to what it was formerly.

There are alternatives to bankruptcy and the consumer should carefully consider them before going bankrupt:

- The consumer debtor may make a deal or enter into a proposal with his or her creditors.

- The consumer debtor may be able to obtain a debt consolidation loan from one bank so that he or she can pay all the other creditors on a minimum monthly payment.

- The consumer debtor may obtain a consolidation order in Small Claims Court, or in some provinces an order directing payments to creditors.

- The consumer debtor's income may increase to cover the carrying charges and pay some principal.

- The consumer debtor's expenses may decrease.

4. Exempt Property

When the consumer debtor goes bankrupt, all of the property that is owned by the debtor and property that the debtor inherits or acquires after bankruptcy up to the time the debtor gets out of bankruptcy automatically belongs to the trustee in bankruptcy without any need or requirement to transfer or register ownership, except for real estate. The trustee in bankruptcy must sell the debtor's eligible or non-exempt property and then distribute the sale proceeds amongst the creditors. Eligible property includes all kinds of property wherever it is whether inside or outside Canada. Property that is acquired by the bankrupt after bankruptcy up to the time of discharge is called "after-acquired" property. It usually includes wages, commissions, inheritances from family members, and winnings from lottery tickets.

However, not all property goes to the trustee. In each province and territory, there are exemptions for bankrupts. These exemptions provide that the consumer debtor, now the bankrupt, can keep certain kinds of property. In other words, creditors cannot seize this type of property. While this is covered a little later in the book, in Chapter 6, the consumer debtor should note that he or she can keep most of the wages, vehicles, tools of the job, generally all clothing, furniture, pension funds, RRSP money with the exception of money deposited within the last year before bankruptcy, insurance proceeds, and proceeds arising out of a personal injury action.

5. Protection Against Lawsuits

Once the consumer debtor is in bankruptcy, a creditor who has a claim provable in the bankruptcy is stopped or prevented from starting any lawsuit or continuing any lawsuit against the bankrupt or the bankrupt's property. The bankruptcy operates as a stay of legal proceedings by most creditors. These creditors have a right to look to what property the bankrupt had at the time of bankruptcy for payment. They are not entitled to take any legal proceedings against the bankrupt except with the permission of the court. This permission is rarely given except in the cases of fraud, misrepresentation, or with respect to the enforcement of a support order or in the case of a motor vehicle claim where there is insurance coverage. Bankruptcy does not stop or stay criminal investigations or contempt proceedings.

Secured creditors can enforce their security against the bankrupt. They do not need the court's permission to repossess the person's property after bankruptcy. For example, a secured creditor could seize the bankrupt's vehicle if payments are in arrears or a secured creditor could foreclose on the bankrupt's home for arrears of mortgage payments or taxes.

Therefore, the bankrupt can be assured that the sheriff or bailiff will not seize his or her assets or take garnishment proceedings without a special court order being made.

5.1 Wage assignments

Many consumer bankrupts give creditors a wage assignment as security for loans. A wage assignment is an agreement between the debtor and the employer which gives the employer the right to deduct amounts from the debtor's wages to pay a creditor who has a judgment. When a consumer debtor goes into bankruptcy, the wage assignment does not continue. Instead, the bankrupt is now required to pay a portion of his or her surplus income to the trustee in bankruptcy for distribution to all the creditors.

5.2 Licences

Sometimes, a consumer debtor may hold a licence under legislation that regulates the industry. For example, a consumer debtor may require a real estate broker's licence, a licence to sell securities, a licence to sell used vehicles, and other types of licences that are issued by provincial and federal governments. Each type of licence has to be reviewed under its applicable legislation to see what happens on bankruptcy. The consumer debtor should consult the governing body that issues and regulates the licence before making an assignment into bankruptcy. Some legislation allows an undischarged bankrupt to continue earning a living while other legislation prohibits the bankrupt from using the licence until there is a discharge. In some cases, a consumer debtor who files an assignment may not be able to obtain a fidelity bond. This may also affect any renewal of the licence. In such a case, the consumer debtor should consider filing a consumer proposal so that the licence can be preserved.

For example, a lawyer who goes bankrupt in Ontario may continue to practise, but an undischarged lawyer in Ontario cannot maintain a trust account. The lawyer must therefore work with another lawyer as such trust accounts are monitored by the Law Society of Upper Canada. However, if a public accountant goes bankrupt, the accountant loses his or her licence during bankruptcy.

Therefore, it is necessary for the consumer debtor to review the legislation governing the licence that is held before making an assignment in bankruptcy as without a licence the consumer debtor may lose his or her job temporarily, and may have some difficulty in getting the licence back after discharge.

6. Costs

In 2000, there were 75,137 consumer bankruptcies in Canada and 12,392 consumer proposals. In 2010, there were a total 135,008 consumer bankruptcies in Canada of which 42,314 made proposals. In 2011, there were a total of 122,999 consumer bankruptcies of which 45,006 made proposals. In most of these consumer bankruptcies, the trustee's fees ran about $1,800 and up. Under the *Bankruptcy and Insolvency Act*, there is a prescribed tariff for trustees in performing services for little- or no-asset bankruptcy estates. If the consumer debtor needs a lawyer, the costs will usually be based on an hourly rate. A consumer debtor should be able to get good competent legal advice on bankruptcy matters for less than $1,500. Of course, if there are special problems, the costs are likely to be higher. Therefore, most consumer debtors should have or be able to raise about $3,300 if they want to use the services of a lawyer and a trustee to go bankrupt.

If the consumer debtor has any doubts about bankruptcy or its effects, it is advisable to see a lawyer first before filing as once the consumer debtor files for bankruptcy, it is virtually impossible to annul or reverse its effect.

If the consumer debtor does not have any assets to pay the trustee or a lawyer, then it is possible that the trustee may obtain a guarantee or a cash retainer from a family member or from a friend of the consumer debtor. The guarantee operates only if the trustee is unable to recover property or realize any monies from the property that the bankrupt earns after bankruptcy up to the time of discharge. The guarantee should be in writing and the guarantor, the family member or friend, should read the guarantee very carefully so that it is understood at what is being signed. Trustees usually require that their money be paid before formal proceedings take place.

It is also possible for the consumer debtor to access the Bankruptcy Assistance Program supervised by the Office of the Superintendent of Bankruptcy if the consumer does not have a family member or friend to assist. However, the consumer must first make attempts to retain the services of two private licensed trustees, not be involved in any commercial businesses, and not have any surplus income. If the consumer debtor qualifies, the consumer debtor can contact the local office of the Superintendent where a bankruptcy analyst will designate a participating trustee to administer the bankruptcy or proposal.

7. Information You Will Need to Share at a Bankruptcy Interview with a Trustee or Lawyer

Bankruptcy laws generally provide that transactions entered into by a debtor within five years of the date of bankruptcy require review by the trustee on behalf of the creditors. The trustee is concerned about property that the consumer debtor had, what the consumer debtor received for it when it was transferred, and where it is today. It is improper, generally, for a consumer debtor to give away property or transfer property at less than its fair value at a time when the consumer debtor is having financial difficulties and cannot readily pay his or her creditors. If the consumer debtor does not have sufficient assets at the time of the transfer or gift, then it is possible that the trustee or the creditors may move to set aside that transfer. If the transfer is set aside, the property re-vests in the name of the consumer debtor and thereafter the trustee or creditors can force its sale. Accordingly, a careful review of all assets should be made within five years of the projected date of bankruptcy. This would include the following:

- ◆ Full particulars about the consumer debtor including:
  - ◇ surname, given names, nicknames
  - ◇ address including postal code
  - ◇ telephone and fax numbers, email addresses
  - ◇ driver's licence number
  - ◇ social insurance number (show card)
  - ◇ date of birth, with birth certificate
  - ◇ passports, citizenship, or landed immigrant papers
  - ◇ marital status, and where appropriate, separation agreement, divorce order, support order
  - ◇ dependents' names, relationship, and ages
  - ◇ occupation

- name of employer including telephone and fax numbers, email address, and postal address
- salary, wages, or other remuneration
- full particulars of spouse, partner, or friend including names, date of birth, and social insurance number
- income tax returns for the last five years

- Full particulars of all assets in Canada and elsewhere, including:
  - cash, bank accounts
  - insurance policies for life and property, and names of beneficiaries and relationship
  - furniture and furnishings
  - securities including stocks, guaranteed investment certificates (GIC), shares of public and private companies
  - bonds, over the last five years including brokerage statements
  - vehicles, licence plates, ownership, and insurance particulars
  - real estate
  - leasehold
  - equipment
  - receivables and IOUs
  - personal assets including collections having a value of more than $500, collections of silver, crystal, gold, coins, liquor, guns, art, and artifacts
  - credit cards
  - copies of net worth statements provided to any bank, lender, or other creditor
  - copies of pass books or bank statements in the consumer debtor's name alone or jointly with others
  - copies of all credit card statements in the consumer debtor's name

- Full particulars of all debts including names of creditors in alphabetical order, addresses, and amounts outstanding.

- RRSP, RRIF, and other pension statements for the last five years including documentation with respect to any change in the names of beneficiaries. The trustee and creditors cannot attach RRSPs except for monies invested within one year of bankruptcy.

- Full particulars of all dispositions and transfers of property within 12 months of taking protection and within 5 years of taking protection.

- Delivery of all credit cards, ownership registrations, mortgages, title deeds, guarantees, insurance policies, tax returns, and all other documents evidencing ownership and debt.

Chapter 2
WHO ARE THE PEOPLE INVOLVED IN A BANKRUPTCY?

As discussed in Chapter 1, a debtor can be an individual person, partnership, or a corporation that is unable to pay debts in the ordinary course. In this chapter, we discuss the other people who are involved in the bankruptcy community including the trustee in bankruptcy, the Superintendent of Bankruptcy or the Office of the Superintendent of Bankruptcy (OSB), the Official Receiver, the Bankruptcy Registrar, and the judge. In all bankruptcies, the consumer debtor comes in contact only with the trustee in bankruptcy. Depending on the nature and size of the bankruptcy, the consumer debtor may come into contact with the other persons referred to in this chapter. The consumer debtor will, of course, have some knowledge about each of the creditors through his or her dealings. Most consumer debtors have many credit cards in their possession and on their Statement of Affairs, they list them with their account numbers, addresses, and debts.

See Figure 1 for a visual of the people involved in a bankruptcy.

Figure I
STRUCTURE

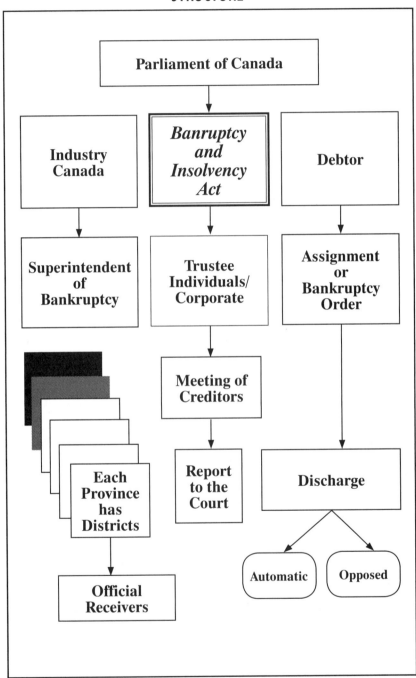

Parliament of Canada

Industry Canada

Banruptcy and Insolvency Act

Debtor

Superintendent of Bankruptcy

Trustee Individuals/ Corporate

Assignment or Bankruptcy Order

Meeting of Creditors

Each Province has Districts

Report to the Court

Discharge

Official Receivers

Automatic

Opposed

I. The Trustee in Bankruptcy (the Administrator)

The trustee in bankruptcy is an individual person or corporation that is licensed by the Superintendent of Bankruptcy under the Department of Industry of the federal government of Canada, referred to as Industry Canada. The trustee's role is to administer the bankrupt's estate, essentially liquidating a debtor's assets and then making a distribution of the sale proceeds to the creditors. It is the trustee in bankruptcy who assists the debtor through this cleansing process.

The trustee has many duties that are described in the *Bankruptcy and the Insolvency Act*. The trustee is usually a person who is a chartered accountant or certified management accountant in private practice, or who is associated with an accounting firm that has a corporate licence to act as a licensed trustee in bankruptcy. The trustee does not, however, have to be a chartered accountant or a certified management accountant. Most of the larger accounting houses in Canada have a bankruptcy department and there are numerous smaller firms and individuals who practise in the bankruptcy field. Most insolvency practitioners are members of the Canadian Association of Insolvency and Restructuring Profession and are given a Chartered Insolvency Restructuring Professional (CIRP) designation to follow their name if they have successfully completed their course of study. As of December 31, 2012, there were approximately 1,000 licensed trustees in Canada.

The trustee is an officer of the court who acts as an intermediary between the debtor and the creditors. While the trustee is appointed to protect the debtor from harassment, the trustee must also assure the creditors that all the debtor's assets have been accounted for and that they have been properly disposed of. The trustee must be even-handed and impartial to both the debtor and the creditors.

The trustee is the person who administers each of the bankruptcy estates. Some of the trustee's responsibilities are to —

- review with the debtor how the bankruptcy process operates;
- interview the debtor with respect to recovering all the debtor's assets including past and present and attaching future assets;
- advise the debtor of his or her duties under the *Bankruptcy and Insolvency Act*;
- call and chair a meeting of creditors when required;

- sell or dispose the assets and then distribute the proceeds according the priorities under the Act;

- report to the creditors generally as to the financial affairs of the bankrupt and on the bankrupt's discharge; and

- counsel the debtor as to the causes of financial problems and how to avoid them in the future. There are three counselling sessions, two of which are mandatory.

In situations where the insolvent person is a consumer, the Superintendent of Bankruptcy has the authority under the *Bankruptcy and Insolvency Act* to appoint any person or a trustee to be an administrator under the Act for bankruptcies and consumer proposals. The administrator need not be a licensed trustee or an accountant. This is useful in remote communities which may not have access to a licensed trustee in bankruptcy. The administrator has all the powers and duties of a trustee in bankruptcy.

2. Different Types of Creditors

Under the *Bankruptcy and Insolvency Act*, there are three general types of creditors.

First, there are **secured creditors**. Secured creditors are types of creditors that hold some form of property as security for the payment of a debt. For example, if a bank holds a mortgage over the debtor's home, the mortgage document creates the security against the home. The consumer debtor cannot sell or transfer the home without paying the bank. If the debtor fails to pay monthly, or fails to pay taxes or other amounts under the mortgage, the bank has the right to foreclose, that is to become the owner, or the bank has the right to sell the home to pay the debt. If the bank does not sell the home for enough money to cover the mortgage debt, then the bank has a shortfall and the amount of that shortfall is an unsecured claim in the bankruptcy.

Consider this example: The Dominion Bank holds a mortgage against the debtor's home for $200,000. There are no other mortgages against the debtor's home. If the debtor defaults in making monthly payments to the bank, the bank has a right through legal process to take the debtor's home and eventually sell it. If the bank realizes $160,000 towards the $200,000 loan, then $40,000 is the shortfall or deficiency. The bank then has an unsecured claim for the $40,000. However, if the bank sells the home for $240,000, the bank has a $40,000 surplus, and the debtor is entitled to that money. If the debtor were bankrupt for other debts, the trustee would intercept the $40,000.

Second, there are the **preferred creditors**. These are certain types of creditors that are specifically recognized under the *Bankruptcy and Insolvency Act*. There are several different types including wage earners, claims under support orders, municipalities for business taxes, and landlords of commercial premises. They receive a preferred place if there is a distribution of monies from the sale of the debtor's assets. Preferred creditors are reviewed in Chapter 5.

Last, there are ordinary **unsecured creditors**. These are creditors who do not hold any of the property of the debtor as security for the debt and they are not given any priority or preferred standing in the administration. One example might be a mobile phone service provider. They have no special rights against the debtor or against his or her property. Creditors who obtain judgment against the debtor are also in this group.

3. The Superintendent of Bankruptcy

The Superintendent of Bankruptcy is a person appointed by the Minister of Industry Canada in Ottawa to supervise the administration of all bankruptcies, receiverships, and other matters to which the *Bankruptcy and Insolvency Act* applies throughout Canada. The Superintendent is appointed as the senior administrator under the Department of Industry and has an office in Ottawa. The Superintendent's role is to review and monitor the performance of all trustees across Canada as well as review debtor compliance with the Act, its rules, and directives. The Superintendent can also become involved, where necessary, with the administration of any bankruptcy or receivership estate where there may be reason to believe that there are irregularities, or for the protection of the public.

The Superintendent of Bankruptcy and staff, called the Office of the Superintendent of Bankruptcy (OSB), review the conduct and practice of all licensed trustees and bankrupts. The Office of the Superintendent keeps statistics of all bankruptcies and proposals for Statistics Canada.

The OSB is the official licensing board for trustees in Canada. All candidates and trustees must obtain a licence from the Superintendent's office before they can administer bankruptcies. The OSB, in conjunction with the Canadian Association of Insolvency and Restructuring Professionals, an association of insolvency professionals throughout Canada, work together in setting up a course for students. Jointly, they prescribe the materials and examinations that a person must perform adequately before a licence is granted. There are both written and oral examinations held at least once a year in major centres across Canada for this purpose. The OSB website is www.ic.gc.ca/eic/site/bsf-osb.nsf/eng/home. The website provides useful information about bankruptcy and insolvency, a trustee directory, resources for additional reading, statistics, and other relevant information. The Superintendent's contact information is set out in Appendix II.

4. The Official Receiver

The Superintendent of Bankruptcy monitors the function and role of trustees through various offices throughout Canada, and is represented by Official Receivers throughout Canada. Each province is a bankruptcy district, and within each district, there may be one or more divisions. Within the division, there are a number of Official Receivers that represent the Superintendent.

Under the *Bankruptcy and Insolvency Act*, the Superintendent and the Official Receivers are required to perform certain tasks during the administration of the bankrupt's estate. For example, the trustee's conduct is monitored by the Official Receiver on behalf of the Superintendent. Any complaint about a trustee is usually given to the Official Receiver in the area where the trustee practises. The Official Receiver chairs the first meeting of creditors in the bankruptcy or under a proposal. However, the Official Receiver can delegate this function to the trustee. Where necessary, the Official Receiver examines the bankrupt or the principal of the bankrupt if it is a corporation concerning the conduct of the bankruptcy, and the disposition of assets that may have been transferred or conveyed before the bankruptcy.

The offices of the Official Receivers are set out in Appendix II.

5. The Bankruptcy Judge

Most consumer debtors who go through the bankruptcy process never appear before the bankruptcy judge. However, if the consumer debtor has been bankrupt before or has been reckless with his or her assets before going into bankruptcy or has incurred significant debt, then it is probable that when the debtor applies to get out, or get discharged, he or she will be required to attend before the registrar or the bankruptcy judge to explain the circumstances surrounding the bankruptcy.

The bankruptcy judge hears many other matters arising out the bankruptcy. One area is that of discharges where the creditors have an opportunity to oppose the debtor's application. Once the debtor is placed into bankruptcy, the trustee has a duty to file for the bankrupt's discharge hearing. There is more about discharges in Chapter 14.

6. The Registrar in Bankruptcy

The registrar in bankruptcy is also a court official. The registrar has the authority to rule and judge certain types of cases. Depending on the need, there is usually only one registrar in each province whose office is close to the superior court in the capital. However, there may be deputy registrars in other cities of the province. The deputies have the same authority as the registrar.

In Ontario, there are two registrars who sit in Toronto; there are also deputy registrars, one in London and the other in Ottawa. In Quebec, there are several registrars located in major centres.

The powers of the registrar are set out in the *Bankruptcy and Insolvency Act*. The registrar can —

- ♦ hear cases where both sides have agreed to some solution of a problem;

- ♦ examine any person under oath who has knowledge of the bankrupt's affairs;

- ♦ grant orders of discharge; that is, once the debtor is in bankruptcy, the debtor will usually want to get out or get "discharged"; that hearing can take place before the registrar;

- ♦ make orders in urgent cases;

- ♦ determine matters relating to proofs of claim; and

- ♦ fix the fees of the trustee and the fees of the lawyer for the trustee.

With respect to discharge hearings, the court administration determines whether the discharge is heard by the registrar or bankruptcy judge. The registrar also has other powers that are of a more technical nature.

7. The Inspectors

Inspectors are persons who represent the creditors and guide the trustee in the deliberations and actions throughout the administration. Once a bankruptcy occurs, there may be a meeting of creditors if requested by the creditors or the trustee. There is seldom a creditors' meeting in consumer bankruptcies. If a meeting is held, the creditors appoint representatives amongst themselves to discuss the bankrupt's financial affairs with the trustee. Those representatives are called inspectors. In most cases, those representatives are present at the first meeting of creditors.

Under the *Bankruptcy and Insolvency Act*, there can be a maximum of five inspectors appointed. Usually, there is an odd number so that a deadlock vote does not occur, although the trustee may vote in the case of a tie. In consumer bankruptcies, there are usually no inspectors since there are no assets or very few assets to administer. Inspectors are paid a nominal amount for each meeting that they attend. Meetings are held to —

- ♦ discuss the method and the mechanics of the sale of the bankrupt's assets,
- ♦ investigate the affairs of the bankrupt,
- ♦ authorize any examination of the bankrupt or others,
- ♦ authorize lawsuits to void transactions, and
- ♦ generally assist the trustee in making decisions.

The trustee relies on the advice of the inspectors since they represent the creditors. They are usually knowledgeable persons who supplied the bankrupt with goods, services, or money, and generally know much about the bankrupt's business and affairs.

8. Others

There are other people who are involved in the bankruptcy process. However, while the debtor may not come into contact with them, the debtor may hear about them throughout the process. For example, there is the bailiff who represents the landlord; the bailiff locks the doors of the tenant debtor if the tenant fails to pay the rent. Then there is the inventory counter, and the liquidator and auctioneer who sells the debtor's assets at an auction or at a private sale.

In both the Official Receiver's office and in the bankruptcy office of the superior court of the province, there are staff members who assist in processing the bankruptcy documents for the public record and assist in conducting searches. They coordinate the times for the court proceedings. In the trustee's office, there are clerks and estate managers who assist the trustee in interviewing and in completing the reports that are required in each bankruptcy estate. Many unseen people are involved.

Chapter 3
TIME SEQUENCE IN THE BANKRUPTCY PROCESS

There are several major steps to processing the bankruptcy paperwork when going through bankruptcy from beginning to end. These steps are highlighted in this chapter. After reading this book or parts of it, the consumer debtor may have questions that are not answered and therefore, should make up a list of questions to ask the trustee in bankruptcy before the papers are signed and filed. In addition, and depending on the consumer debtor's particular problems, the consumer debtor may want to see a lawyer first who has experience in this area, or an accountant who may have a general background in dealing with bankruptcy and insolvency situations. The consumer debtor should definitely consult a lawyer before the papers are signed and filed because once they are filed with the Official Receiver's office, the lawyer will not likely be able to reverse the process and the lawyer's advice as to whether the bankruptcy route was proper will be too late.

As mentioned in previous chapters, there are ways to avoid bankruptcy including negotiating with the creditors on an informal basis or making a formal proposal under the *Bankruptcy and Insolvency Act*. These and other choices are discussed further in Chapter 9.

For a visual of the time sequence involved in bankruptcy, see Figure 2.

I. Contact a Trustee

Once bankruptcy is chosen, contact a trustee. A trustee is licensed from the federal government under the *Bankruptcy and Insolvency Act* to assist and prepare the papers for bankruptcy on behalf of individuals, partnerships, and corporations. The consumer debtor can contact a trustee at several different sources. Many large accounting firms throughout Canada have divisions or separate corporations dealing with bankruptcy and related matters. As such, they will have a corporate licence to deal with bankruptcies. Larger accounting firms may not have a department that deals with consumer bankrupcies. Intermediate and smaller accounting firms and even smaller partnerships and sole proprietors will have licences from the federal government to administer bankruptcies. These firms will be able to handle a consumer bankruptcy.

Alternatively, the consumer debtor may be referred to a trustee through his or her own accountant or lawyer, or the debtor may have heard about a particular trustee through online advertising, free newspapers, word of mouth, and in the Yellow Pages online or in print. While all trustees are qualified and have the same licence, some trustees deal with specialty areas while others do not. For example, a sole practitioner may deal only with consumer bankruptcies whereas a large accounting firm may not deal with consumers at all, but with business restructurings, or perhaps both. Where possible, it is always best to go to a trustee that has been recommended by another person: lawyer, accountant, or friend.

When selecting a trustee, it is important to feel compatible with the person with whom the consumer debtor is working. The trustee's role is to assist the debtor in this bankruptcy process and to make sure that the debtor goes through the bankruptcy process with as less discomfort as possible. However, the trustee is not the consumer debtor's friend. The trustee is an officer of the court under the Act to represent both the consumer debtor and the creditors. In other words, the trustee must be even-handed with both the consumer debtor and the creditors. The trustee has a job to perform that may conflict with the consumer debtor's expectations. Sometimes, personality conflicts may arise and once the bankruptcy proceedings have started, it is very unlikely that the consumer debtor can switch to another trustee.

Figure 2
TIME SEQUENCE

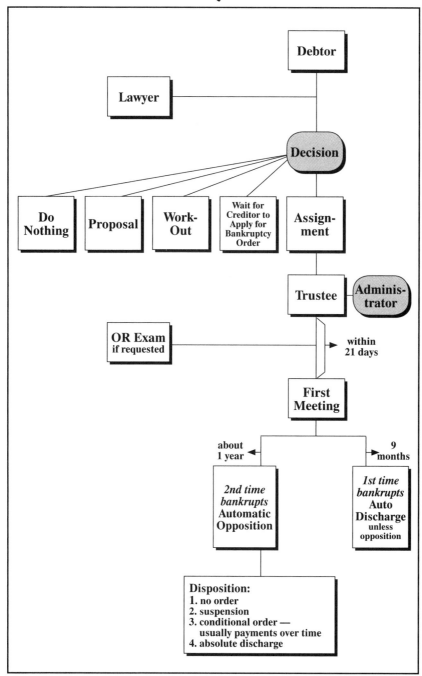

For the average consumer bankruptcy, going to a recommended professional may not amount to much difference. But in more complicated matters, an individual will want the relationship to be compatible rather than confrontational. If the consumer debtor has or anticipates problems with respect to taking bankruptcy protection, the consumer debtor should see a lawyer first.

The consumer debtor should also shop around for the cost of the trustee's services. While all the trustees have the same duties to perform, some charge more. For consumer bankruptcies, the fees and disbursements, or costs, could range from $1,500 to about $3,000. The cost varies depending on the number of visits that the debtor makes to the trustee's office, the duration of those visits, the experience of the people handling the case, the number of creditors that have to be notified, the problems relating to the debtor's assets, the determination of exempt assets, the level of income, and other factors. Often, the consumer debtor does not have all the bills, invoices, and statements needed to prepare the forms. Obtaining these documents may take some additional time and therefore increase the fees.

These costs are paid from the consumer debtor's bank account if there are sufficient monies to cover them, or they can come from the sale proceeds of the debtor's assets or from third party guarantors. The amount of costs is also controlled under the Act. The trustee must have its costs reviewed or taxed by the registrar when it applies for its own discharge. Some trustees allow the consumer debtor to pay a monthly sum until the bill is paid. If the consumer debtor does not pay the full amount of the bill by the discharge date (nine months from the date the papers are filed with the Official Receiver), the trustee may oppose the application in which case the discharge will be delayed. While courts frown on this practice, the consumer debtor should be aware that his or her discharge may be delayed if he or she does not pay the trustee in full, on time.

Once the consumer debtor has made the initial contact with the trustee, the trustee or his or her assistant requires the debtor to meet and review all the assets and liabilities. That means the consumer debtor will be asked many questions about —

♦ what the consumer debtor had (i.e., assets the debtor did own over the last five years, but has since sold or transferred or gave away to other persons);

♦ what the consumer debtor has (i.e., assets the debtor presently owns, uses, or has an interest in); and

♦ what the consumer debtor might have in the future (i.e., monies the debtor may receive by way of salary, wages, or other remuneration, on an insurance claim, other lawsuits, or through an inheritance).

These questions are designed to disclose assets that may be available for realization from which the proceeds would be distributed to the creditors. From this information, the trustee prepares a Statement of Affairs. The completion of the forms is discussed later in this book.

Some questions point out possible problems that the consumer debtor may have with the creditors or in dealing with some of the assets. For example, the consumer debtor may want to know if he or she can keep a vehicle or whether the debtor will lose his or her investments in an RRSP. These are difficult questions which the trustee may not be able to answer readily. It is at this point in time (i.e., when some questions remain unanswered) that it is best to hire or retain a lawyer to assist, hopefully before the consumer debtor takes bankruptcy protection. If the trustee points out some difficulties, the consumer debtor should seek legal advice first from a lawyer. For example, if the consumer debtor has high earnings, the trustee will require the debtor to pay a portion of his or her earnings monthly to the trustee for all the creditors or if the consumer debtor has transferred the car to his daughter within the last three weeks, the daughter may have to transfer it back or pay the trustee the value.

Whether or not the consumer debtor will be aware of these problems is a different matter. If the trustee does not tell the consumer debtor that there are problems, then these problems may arise while the debtor is in bankruptcy or when the debtor wants to get out of bankruptcy or get discharged. This is the reason a consumer debtor may want to see a lawyer first before going bankrupt as the consumer debtor may decide not to go bankrupt at that time, or at any time.

If the trustee recognizes complications in an interview, then the trustee may suggest a consultation with a lawyer. At that time, the lawyer may point out the problems in dealing with certain assets that the consumer debtor owns as well as with the types of creditors that may be hostile and adverse throughout the bankruptcy process. Unlike the trustee, the consumer debtor can tell the lawyer everything about his or her personal affairs on a confidential and private basis. Communications between the consumer debtor (the client) and the lawyer are protected by law, and the lawyer must not breach that confidence. In fact, what the consumer debtor says to the lawyer is privileged and confidential and generally, with the exception of fraud and locating assets, no one can make the lawyer divulge that information and the legal advice given without the consumer debtor's consent. However, such privilege does not extend to third parties, such as spouses, friends, and accountants, who attend the lawyer's office with the consumer debtor.

2. File an Assignment

If the consumer debtor wishes to proceed with the bankruptcy process, the debtor eventually signs a form called an "Assignment." The Assignment form is a one-page document that transfers all the debtor's assets to the trustee under the *Bankruptcy and Insolvency Act*. It is the document that puts the consumer debtor into bankruptcy by his or her own hand (voluntarily). An example of this form is shown in Chapter 12.

In addition to the Assignment, the consumer debtor also signs a Statement of Affairs, a "pertinent information sheet," and a Personal Income and Expense Statement. The Statement of Affairs, also shown in Chapter 12, is the document that sets out all the consumer debtor's assets and all the liabilities with full particulars. In the liabilities section, the consumer debtor names all the creditors to whom the debtor owes money. The pertinent information sheet contains many questions about the consumer debtor's present status and about previous dealings with property.

When these documents are signed, they are then e-filed by the trustee to the Official Receiver, a government officer, in the area which the consumer debtor resides for filing. Alternatively, the trustee may fax or deliver the documents to the office for filing. (The government offices are listed in Appendix II.) Once these documents are accepted by the Official Receiver, the consumer debtor is then officially bankrupt.

3. Attend an Examination by the Official Receiver

Once the consumer debtor is bankrupt, the debtor is required to perform a number of duties. These are set out in more detail in Chapter 8. One of the duties is to attend, if requested by the creditors or by the Superintendent of Bankruptcy, or by the office of the Official

Receiver, an examination as to the consumer's debtor's assets and liabilities before the first meeting of creditors.

In consumer bankruptcies, there is seldom an examination. However, where the trustee suspects credit card abuse, extravagant living, or gambling, the trustee may call the Official Receiver and request that the Official Receiver conduct an examination. The trustee and the Official Receiver usually set the date and time of the examination, but it is usually held shortly before the first meeting of creditors, if one is requested. The consumer debtor, now bankrupt, must attend and answer questions under oath concerning the debtor's conduct before bankruptcy, the causes of bankruptcy, and the disposition of the debtor's property over the last five years. Many of the questions are of a general nature.

On occasion, the Official Receiver obtains information from the trustee and the creditors, and then makes up some new questions relating to the debtor's property. The Official Receiver's questionnaire is designed to bring out answers relating to the debtor's assets that the debtor may have had prior to bankruptcy so that the trustee and the creditors may recover these assets that have been conveyed improperly to friends, family, and business associates. The consumer debtor usually attends the meeting without a lawyer, but may bring a lawyer or friend to assist; it is not usual for the consumer debtor to bring a lawyer to this type of examination. In fact, if the debtor brings a lawyer, the Official Receiver may suspect that there may be problems in the administration. Unlike at the Official Receiver's examination, the bankrupt is not under oath when attending the first meeting of creditors.

The Official Receiver usually writes the answers on the form, and on additional pages if necessary. At the end of the examination, the Official Receiver asks the consumer debtor to review the answers and sign the form under oath. The consumer debtor should read the material carefully and make any corrections at that time, or as soon as the debtor realizes an error.

At the meeting of creditors, the Official Receiver reads the answers aloud. Creditors may ask additional questions at that time.

4. Attend the First Meeting of Creditors

In consumer bankruptcies, there is not likely to be a meeting of creditors unless requested. Within 30 days of the bankruptcy, the

Official Receiver or creditors having at least 25 percent in value of the proven claims can request a meeting of creditors. If a creditors' meeting is requested, the trustee must send a notice of bankruptcy and notice of impending automatic discharge for first-time bankrupts to creditors. The notice must indicate the amount of surplus income that the bankrupt is required to pay the estate.

If a meeting is requested, it must be held within 21 days after being called. If a meeting is called, it is usually because the consumer debtor owes substantial money to creditors, or credit card issuers suspect something improper or illegal.

If the Official Receiver or creditors wish to call a meeting, the trustee in bankruptcy must notify all the creditors of the date, time, and location for the first meeting of creditors in the bankruptcy estate. The Official Receiver sets the date and time and usually confers with the trustee in doing this.

The trustee sends a notice of the first meeting with the statement of affairs and a summary list of creditors to all the creditors, advising them of the date, time, and location of the first meeting of creditors, and advising them that if they wish to come and vote, they must first file a proof of claim before the meeting begins. If the trustee does not accept the proof of claim, the creditor will not be permitted to vote.

While not usual for consumer bankruptcies, the Official Receiver's examination of the bankrupt is usually held the day before or during the morning before the first meeting of creditors. At the first meeting of creditors (and usually there is only one as second or subsequent meetings can become expensive), the Official Receiver and trustee review a number of matters including the results of the examination and then the trustee obtains directions from the creditors. This is covered in more detail in Chapter 5.

5. Apply to the Court for a Discharge

The bankruptcy of an individual person operates as an application for discharge. If the bankrupt is a first-time bankrupt, then there is an automatic discharge nine months after filing unless the bankrupt has refused or neglected to receive counselling or where a creditor, the trustee, or the Superintendent objects to the discharge, or where the bankrupt has no surplus income. If there is opposition, there is a special hearing before the bankruptcy registrar or judge. For individuals who have been bankrupt before, or in circumstances where their conduct is questionable, the discharge could take much longer.

While the consumer debtor is undischarged, that is while the consumer debtor is still in bankruptcy, the consumer debtor's surplus wages, salary, or commission, or a draw as a self-employed individual, are subject to seizure or attachment by the trustee for the benefit of creditors. The amount that the trustee is entitled to attach depends on the debtor's family income, family responsibilities, and personal situation. On filing the bankruptcy papers, the trustee must review the consumer debtor's surplus income requirement and determine according to the Superintendent's Standards what portion the debtor is going to pay to the estate while the debtor is undischarged. Annually, the Superintendent's office publishes these standards in chart form setting out suggested payments depending upon the size of income and the number of dependents. The standards are the same across Canada and do not take into account regional disparities of income and expenses; see Appendix III.

At the discharge hearing, creditors may oppose the consumer debtor's discharge if they have reason to believe that the debtor's conduct prior to and during the bankruptcy was improper under certain prescribed provisions of the *Bankruptcy and Insolvency Act*. When the consumer debtor gets out of bankruptcy all the proceedings stop and the consumer debtor is free to enter into business and obtain credit once again.

In Chapter 14, there is a review of the discharge hearing and what a consumer debtor can expect at the hearing.

Figure 3 shows the bankruptcy process.

Figure 3
BANKRUPTCY PROCESS

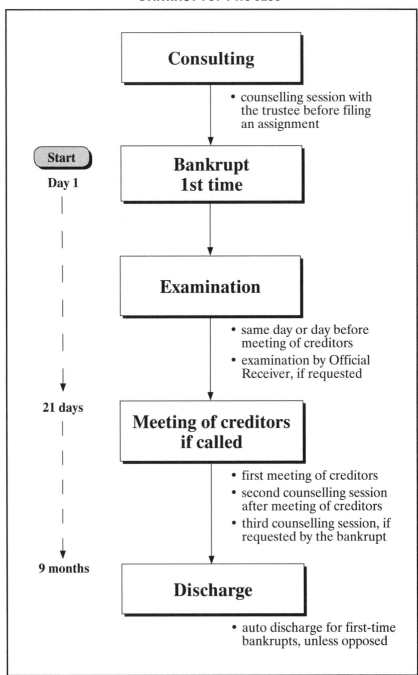

Consulting

- counselling session with the trustee before filing an assignment

Start
Day 1

Bankrupt 1st time

Examination

- same day or day before meeting of creditors
- examination by Official Receiver, if requested

21 days

Meeting of creditors if called

- first meeting of creditors
- second counselling session after meeting of creditors
- third counselling session, if requested by the bankrupt

9 months

Discharge

- auto discharge for first-time bankrupts, unless opposed

Chapter 4
WHAT IS THE ROLE OF THE TRUSTEE?

This chapter discusses what the trustee in bankruptcy does in the bankruptcy process.

The trustee acts as an intermediary between the consumer debtor and the creditors. The trustee's job is to gather in all the consumer debtor's non-exempt assets, obtain the maximum amount of money from the sale of the assets, attach surplus income while the consumer debtor is undischarged, and then distribute the monies to all the creditors in a prescribed formula set out under the *Bankruptcy and Insolvency Act*. Further, the trustee has special powers of investigation and examination, and has special rights to sue persons or companies that may be improperly holding the consumer debtor's property or may have received the consumer debtor's property for little or no value. When an undischarged bankrupt applies for a discharge, the trustee files a report with respect to the consumer debtor's financial affairs and his or her conduct before and after bankruptcy. This is called a Section 170 Report. The court carefully considers the trustee's report on the discharge hearing. The trustee's role is to remain even-handed or fair-handed in dealing with the consumer debtor and the creditors. The trustee, as an officer of the court, must not take positions that prejudice either side.

1. Trustee's Responsibilities

The following sections discuss the trustee's responsibilities.

1.1 Counsels the consumer debtor and prepares the forms

If the debtor is a consumer debtor or an employee of a company, the debtor may not choose to see a lawyer first before going bankrupt. The consumer debtor can find a licensed trustee in bankruptcy in the Yellow Pages or in newspaper advertising, or by referral from a lawyer, an accountant, or a friend. Debtors should make an appointment to see the trustee to discuss first, whether the consumer debtor should make an assignment (i.e., go bankrupt) and at the same time obtain counselling services as to causes of the financial difficulties, and second, whether the trustee sees any problems if the consumer debtor decides to file an assignment into bankruptcy. If the trustee points out some difficulties, such as where the debtor recently transferred property to a relative for little in exchange, the consumer debtor should immediately consult a lawyer for advice and direction. If the consumer debtor does not see a lawyer before filing the assignment, it is possible that the trustee, or creditors, may sue the relative in order to recover the property and oppose the discharge.

Insofar as the counselling and forms are concerned, the consumer debtor will, **with the assistance of the trustee** or assistant —

- prepare a statement of assets and liabilities with specific information about each entry;
- prepare a detailed monthly budget showing all income and all expenses;
- discuss the consumer debtor's views concerning immediate problems;
- review the various options available including settlements directly with the creditors, proposals, and bankruptcy;
- learn about various legal terms; and
- learn what happens on discharge.

The trustee will interview the consumer debtor with the intent of seeking out information corresponding to the forms that the debtor signs. (The debtor signs (1) an Assignment and (2) a Statement of Affairs including the pertinent information sheet, and (3) a detailed monthly budget.) If the consumer debtor sees a lawyer, the lawyer can also prepare the forms for execution.

The actual Assignment form is a simple one-page document that effectively transfers to the trustee in bankruptcy all the consumer debtor's property, subject to certain exemptions. These exemptions are set out in Chapter 6.

The consumer debtor must also complete a Statement of Affairs with the trustee or lawyer. A Statement of Affairs is a document that lists all the consumer debtor's assets wherever they may be found, whether in Canada or elsewhere. There are ten different categories of assets with appropriate space for their description and estimated dollar value.

The consumer debtor will complete the list of liabilities by naming the creditors to whom money is owing. The information will contain the names, addresses, account numbers, and amounts owed to each creditor. In addition to the list of assets and the list of liabilities, the consumer debtor will complete a one-page sheet containing pertinent information to his or her affairs. This is reviewed in more detail in Chapter 12.

Once these forms are completed and signed, the lawyer or trustee can then file them in the Bankruptcy District Office of the Superintendent. When they are filed, the Office affixes a stamp on the Assignment with the date, and that is the date of bankruptcy for all purposes under the *Bankruptcy and Insolvency Act* and other legislation that provides for bankruptcy. The bankruptcy is recognized across Canada and internationally.

1.2 Administers the Estate

Once the trustee files the Assignment in bankruptcy with the Official Receiver, the trustee has then many duties to perform for the creditors and the court. In smaller estates, where the realizable assets are less than $15,000, the trustee operates under the summary administration provisions of the *Bankruptcy and Insolvency Act*. This means, for one thing, that the trustee does not publish a notice of the bankruptcy in the local newspaper. The summary administration provisions also permit the trustee to save costs in the administration and allow the trustee to proceed to administer the estate without having inspector approval (i.e., the approval of creditors who wish to assist and direct the trustee). Most consumer bankruptcies are administered under the summary administration provisions of the Act.

In administering the estate, the trustee performs the following main duties:

- Takes possession of the consumer debtor's property and records as soon as possible.

- Verifies an inventory.

- Collects credit cards.

- Obtains an appraisal of the assets.

- Sells or disposes of property.

- Obtains legal advice, if necessary.

- Insures the property.

- Commences legal proceedings to collect monies that are owing.

- Engages the consumer debtor to assist in the administration.

- Intercepts the consumer debtor's mail, but only with an order of the court.

- Reports to the creditors, the Superintendent, and the court.

- Conducts the first and second counselling sessions (first is usually at intake; second within seven months of bankruptcy).

1.3 Reports to the Creditors

One of the duties that the trustee is required to perform under the Act is to become informed of the names and addresses of the creditors and within five business days of the appointment, send a notice calling the first meeting of creditors. For the consumer debtor, there may not be a meeting of creditors. If a meeting is called, it is usually held within three weeks of the appointment. In some cases, the trustee may obtain an order from the registrar, deputy registrar, or judge extending the time to send the notices of the first meeting. In effect, the trustee can delay the meeting until such time as the trustee has been able to assemble the documents and complete the first report.

Aside from the preliminary report to the creditors, the trustee is required to report on request to any creditor and the Superintendent of Bankruptcy.

1.4 Conducts Special Investigations

In completing the Statement of Affairs, the consumer debtor must reveal all transactions dealing with his or her property within the five years leading up to bankruptcy. This information is very important to the trustee, and to the creditors, since the trustee in bankruptcy is given special rights to recover property improperly given away for little or nothing in return.

It is improper for a debtor who is insolvent to deal with his or her property in such a way as to hide or shelter the property from the creditors hoping that on discharge the property will be given back.

Consider this example: If the consumer debtor, knowing that she is having financial problems, transfers her fully paid car to her son within one year prior to bankruptcy, the trustee will want to investigate this transaction and then bring a lawsuit against the son to recover the car if a nominal amount of money was paid.

Or this example: If the consumer debtor, knowing that he is having financial problems, transfers his interest in his family home to his wife or partner within one year prior to bankruptcy, the trustee will want to investigate this transaction and then bring a lawsuit against the wife or partner if a nominal amount of money was paid.

In order to obtain this information, and in situations where the trustee cannot get the information voluntarily, the trustee is given the power to conduct an examination of the bankrupt or any person reasonably thought to have knowledge of the affairs of the bankrupt. The trustee does not require an order of the court before the trustee can examine the bankrupt or anyone who has knowledge of the bankrupt's affairs. The trustee can examine the wife or partner in the above example. The trustee may even examine the debtor's lawyer or accountant.

1.5 Reports to the Court on the Discharge

The trustee in bankruptcy is required to report to the court in a prescribed form with respect to —

♦ the affairs of the bankrupt;

- the causes of the bankruptcy;
- the manner in which the bankrupt has performed the duties under the Act;
- the conduct of the bankrupt both before, during, and after the bankruptcy;
- whether the bankrupt has been convicted of any offence under the Act; and
- any other fact, matter, or circumstance which would justify the court in refusing the bankrupt an unconditional discharge.

If the trustee makes a statement that is incorrect, the consumer debtor has the opportunity to correct it at the hearing. The trustee's report is considered carefully by the court in deciding whether to grant the discharge to the undischarged bankrupt. The procedure on discharge is covered in Chapter 14.

Chapter 5
WHAT ARE THE TYPES OF CREDITORS INVOLVED IN A BANKRUPTCY?

Once the consumer debtor has made an assignment into bankruptcy or a creditor has obtained a bankruptcy order against the debtor, the trustee in bankruptcy must set the administration of the estate into motion. (In an assignment, voluntary, the debtor chooses the trustee. If there is a bankruptcy order, the creditor who initiates the proceeding chooses the trustee.)

In the case of an assignment, the trustee will already have the names and addresses of the creditors. In the case of a bankruptcy order, the trustee has to find out the names and addresses of the creditors within five days of the appointment so that the trustee can send notices calling the first meeting of creditors if required. The consumer bankrupt must meet with the trustee and review the names and addresses of the creditors.

Once the trustee has this information, the trustee can call the first meeting of creditors if requested by the creditors or by the Superintendent. At the first meeting, the trustee reports to the creditors about taking possession of the consumer bankrupt's assets, reviews any examination taken by the Official Receiver, and generally takes direction from the creditors. This chapter covers the immediate administration of a bankruptcy and the types of creditors involved.

1. What Are the Different Types of Creditors?

The consumer bankrupt must advise the trustee in bankruptcy of the names of creditors, addresses, and amounts that are owing to them so that the trustee can prepare and forward the notice of the first meeting of creditors if a meeting is called. As indicated in Chapter 2, there are three main classes of creditors that are recognized under the *Bankruptcy and Insolvency Act*. They are secured creditors, preferred creditors, and unsecured creditors.

1.1 Secured creditors

Secured creditors are creditors who hold some form of property as security for the repayment of debt. Secured creditors include the bank or other lender of money who takes a mortgage on the consumer debtor's home, or a chattel mortgage or security agreement against a person's vehicle, or other personal property. A secured creditor can be a construction lien claimant or the renovator to the consumer debtor's home or even a pawn shop where the consumer debtor has taken his or her musical instrument in return for cash. These creditors look to the property that they hold or have a charge against the property if the consumer debtor fails to pay. In most cases, the secured creditor hopes that the value of the property exceeds the loan and therefore, these secured creditors do not participate in the bankruptcy proceedings for the portion that is unsecured.

1.2 Preferred creditors

Certain types of creditors are named preferred creditors under the *Bankruptcy and Insolvency Act*. While these creditors do not enjoy the security of secured creditors against specific property, they are entitled to a priority of payment ahead of unsecured creditors, but after secured creditors, out of the proceeds of realization from the assets. These preferred creditors comprise those who are owed —

- ♦ funeral expenses in the case where the consumer bankrupt dies before bankruptcy,
- ♦ costs of the administration in the bankruptcy which include trustee's fees and legal costs,

- the levy (a tax on distribution) in favour of the Superintendent which is a 5 percent tax on all payments made to creditors, and

- support claims for amounts owed during the year prior to bankruptcy and any lump sum that may be payable.

1.3 Unsecured creditors

Unsecured or ordinary creditors as they are called do not have any special status under the *Bankruptcy and Insolvency Act.* They are creditors who are owed money for supplying goods or services to the consumer debtor, creditors who are owed deficiency balances after the secured creditor sells the debtor's property, and even creditors who have taken legal proceedings to collect the debt. Creditors who have sued but not recovered judgments, or creditors who have recovered judgments, or have recovered judgments and attempted to enforce the judgments, are in no better position than the other unsecured creditors. Judgment creditors are simply unsecured creditors. If the consumer debtor has student debts from loans from the government, they too are included.

If a consumer debtor has non-exempt assets, the trustee in bankruptcy must first take possession and then sell them. From the sale proceeds, the trustee pays the balances owing to secured creditors, such as mortgages on houses. If there is a surplus left over, then that surplus is distributed to the preferred creditors in the order of priority. If there are not sufficient proceeds flowing down the list, then the creditor next in line does not receive anything. If there are surplus proceeds after payment of all preferred creditors, then the trustee pays the balance to all unsecured creditors on a pro rata or proportionate basis.

Here is an example: Let's say the consumer debtor owns his home with a $200,000 mortgage against it. When the consumer debtor goes bankrupt, the home is worth more than the mortgage and subsequently sells for $260,000 net of real estate fees, legal expenses, and all other expenses. If the debtor is married and his spouse owns one-half of the house, then the trustee in bankruptcy is entitled to $30,000 rather than the $60,000 if the consumer debtor owned the home alone. If the trustee's and legal fees are $10,000, then the difference, being $20,000, is available to all unsecured creditors on a pro rata basis; that is, subtract the preferred claims first from the sale proceeds. That leaves ($30,000-$10,000 = $20,000) available for distribution. If the consumer debtor owes all other creditors $70,000, then each creditor is entitled to a proportionate interest, or as in the example, $0.29 on the dollar outstanding to each creditor less the 5 percent levy to the Superintendent of Bankruptcy.

That is how the distribution works.

1.4 Special Crown claims

In small-business bankruptcies, the bankrupt whether an individual or a corporation will have employees. Canada Revenue Agency (CRA) is a special creditor for unpaid source deductions. The CRA is the beneficiary of "deemed trusts" for the employees' portion of Canada Pension, employment premiums, and income tax deductions. In a situation where the business failed to deduct, or remit payments, corresponding federal legislation imposes or makes the business's assets subject to those trusts. These deemed trusts have priority over all assets of the bankrupt including, in most cases, over the rights of secured creditors. Self-employed and small-business debtors should be aware of these special trust claims. If the assets are not sufficient to pay these taxes, the CRA may proceed against the directors of the company. This, in itself, will usually precipitate a bankruptcy of the directors unless they are able to show that they acted in good faith and with due diligence.

2. When Is the First Meeting of Creditors?

In the case of a consumer bankruptcy, there may not be a meeting of creditors at all. If the bankrupt has no realizable assets that do not exceed $15,000, the trustee can take advantage of the summary administration provisions under the Act. In this case, the trustee does not generally have to publish a notice of the bankruptcy in a local newspaper nor does the trustee have to call a meeting of creditors unless it is requested by the Official Receiver or by the creditors having at least 25 percent of the claims. If a meeting is called, the meeting usually takes place at the trustee's office within 21 days after being called. If the trustee expects many creditors to show up, the trustee will change the place of the meeting to a hall or hotel where there is more room. In many consumer bankruptcies, creditors rarely show up. There are never any assets of value and if there were, they would be subject to some form of security. As a result, there is seldom a meeting of creditors.

However, if the consumer debtor has had a small business, the trustee will notify all the creditors of a meeting. The trustee mails a notice to the creditors advising them of the date, time, and place of the first meeting of the bankruptcy estate. The meeting is to be scheduled for a date usually 21 days after the debtor has gone bankrupt.

If a creditor wants to vote, the creditor must file the proof of claim and voting letter with the trustee before the meeting begins. Many creditors often send their proofs of claim into the trustee's office beforehand. It is also possible to send a proof of claim to the trustee by fax or email.

3. What Happens at the First Meeting of Creditors?

If a meeting of creditors is called in a consumer bankruptcy, the purpose of the first meeting of creditors is fourfold:

1. At the meeting, the creditors and the trustee can discuss all aspects of the consumer bankrupt's affairs. This review generally covers a full discussion of the consumer bankrupt's assets and any dispositions of property made within the last five years from the date of bankruptcy. If the consumer bankrupt transferred property for little or no value within the five-year period at a time when the consumer bankrupt may have been in financial difficulties, then the trustee in bankruptcy may take proceedings to reclaim the property.

2. The creditors affirm the appointment of the trustee. If the creditors do not want the person or corporation named as trustee, they have the right to replace or substitute another trustee in place by a special resolution (i.e., majority of creditors having at least three-fourths in value of the creditors with proven claims). This happens on occasion where the creditors feel that the trustee may not be fully impartial. The creditors likely will have contacted another trustee in bankruptcy before the meeting and they would come armed with the votes to defeat the consumer debtor's choice of trustee.

3. The meeting is held to appoint inspectors. They are individuals usually representing some of the consumer debtor's larger creditors. The inspectors have certain duties to perform. The inspectors assist the trustee in performing the trustee's duties and advise the trustee on difficult problems on realization and review of claims. In exercising their judgment, the inspectors

are making decisions on behalf of all creditors. They receive a nominal fee for their assistance. It is not common to have inspectors in consumer bankruptcies.

4. The meeting gives the creditors the opportunity to air their concerns about the debtor's conduct and an opportunity to give the trustee general directions with respect to the administration of the estate, and particularly as to what they want to do with the assets of the consumer bankrupt and any investigations. In most consumer or small debtor bankruptcies, there are very few assets except, perhaps for a vehicle, a home of minimum equity, and some personal effects exceeding the exemptions. The inspectors and creditors give the trustee general guidance as to what they want to do with these assets.

The Official Receiver chairs the meeting. In consumer bankruptcies, the trustee acts as the Official Receiver's nominee. The Official Receiver, or trustee, advises the meeting of creditors that the bankruptcy documents comply with the requirements under the Act and that everyone who is present is entitled to look at the documents that have been filed under the Act. These documents are:

- The Assignment that was signed by the consumer debtor together with the Statement of Affairs.

- The certificate appointing the trustee named in the Assignment by the Official Receiver.

- An affidavit by the trustee or someone in the trustee's office stating that the notice of the first meeting of creditors was mailed to all creditors and to the consumer bankrupt.

- An affidavit showing that the trustee advertised the fact of bankruptcy in a local newspaper in an ordinary administration if it is a small-business bankruptcy. (In consumer bankruptcies, the publication of the notice of bankruptcy is not required.)

- The Official Receiver's questionnaire of the consumer bankrupt, if taken.

- The trustee's preliminary report as to the investigation into the assets and liabilities of the consumer bankrupt.

These documents are readily available for any creditor to inspect at that time or subsequently.

If the consumer bankrupt has been required to complete the questionnaire, the Official Receiver reviews the questions and answers and then requests questions from the creditors present at the meeting. The bankrupt is required to answer; although, he or she is not under oath. Then, the Official Receiver asks that the trustee review the report. Last, the Official Receiver calls for a vote for the approval of the trustee's appointment. In smaller bankruptcy estates, there is seldom a turnout of creditors, and as a general rule, the named trustee in the Assignment continues to act as trustee in bankruptcy even if there are no creditors present.

In more contentious bankruptcy estates, it is possible for the creditors to contest not only the bankruptcy proceedings but also the named trustee, and in those cases, the trustee might be substituted by another trustee.

In addition to these matters, the Official Receiver calls on the creditors present to appoint inspectors. As referred to earlier, these inspectors guide the trustee and are usually the representatives of the larger creditors as they have an interest in the maximum realization from the estate. However, an inspector need not be a creditor.

As well as the affirmation of the appointment of the trustee and the appointment of the inspectors, the trustee and Official Receiver become involved in a general discussion of the affairs of the consumer bankrupt. After a full discussion, the meeting is adjourned and then the inspectors meet with the trustee to discuss and resolve any issues relating to the sale of assets or recovery of assets that might be available.

As a matter of practice, there is seldom a second meeting of creditors in any consumer or small-business bankruptcy.

Chapter 6
WHAT PROPERTY CAN THE CONSUMER DEBTOR KEEP?

When a consumer debtor goes into bankruptcy, that is, when an Assignment and Statement of Affairs are filed with the Official Receiver's office, the consumer debtor loses the capacity or the right to deal with what was once the consumer debtor's assets and property. On bankruptcy, the property of a consumer debtor automatically becomes the property of the trustee in bankruptcy for distribution amongst the creditors. There is no invoice, transfer, or bill of sale from the debtor to the trustee. The transfer is automatic under the *Bankruptcy and Insolvency Act* with the filing of the Assignment with the Official Receiver. There are, however, a few exceptions to this rule including the transfer of real property, and these exceptions are discussed in this chapter.

1. Property the Trustee Is Entitled to Take

On the filing of the papers with the Official Receiver's office, the trustee in bankruptcy is given power under the *Bankruptcy and Insolvency Act* to take possession of the consumer debtor's property, books, and records, and then is given the power to liquidate or sell the property and distribute the proceeds according to the priorities set out in the Act. The priorities provide that the trustee in bankruptcy must pay the proceeds first to secured creditors, then to preferred creditors, and last to unsecured creditors (as discussed in Chapter 5). Trust property never belongs to the bankrupt, and therefore, does not form part of the proceeds for distribution to creditors.

"Property" is defined in the *Bankruptcy and Insolvency Act* to "include property of every description, whether personal property or real property, present or future and wherever the property is located, whether in Canada or elsewhere." Under the Act, the property of the now bankrupt comprises all property wherever the property is located at the date of bankruptcy and such property that the consumer bankrupt acquires before discharge. However, property does not include property that the consumer bankrupt holds in trust for others, such as an RESP for a child. It also does not include exempt property, namely, property that is exempt from execution under federal and provincial statutes and at common law. So, the trustee in bankruptcy is entitled to two types of property relating to the date of bankruptcy.

1.1 Property that the consumer debtor has at the time of filing

The trustee in bankruptcy is entitled to property the debtor has at the time of filing, such as cash in the bank, an interest in a mutual fund, a joint interest in the ownership of the matrimonial home, a valuable stamp collection, a vehicle, shares in a public or private company, and a condominium in Florida. The consumer debtor can retain all RRSPs and RRIFs apart from monies contributed within 12 months of the bankruptcy. With the exception of real estate, the trustee does not have to do anything to become owner of the property. If real estate is involved, the trustee must register a document certifying the appointment in the land registry system which tells anyone who searches the public record that there has been a change of ownership, even though the trustee in bankruptcy automatically becomes the owner on filing of the assignment. The trustee in bankruptcy must take this additional step to protect the interest for the creditors.

1.2 Property that the consumer bankrupt will acquire between the date of bankruptcy and the date of discharge

The trustee in bankruptcy is entitled to property the bankrupt will acquire between filing the assignment and discharge, such as surplus wages, a bonus, salary and commissions, lottery winnings, lawsuits, and an inheritance from a family member who passed away before the debtor's discharge.

Following bankruptcy, the trustee in bankruptcy can require the bankrupt's employer pay a portion of the bankrupt's salary on a regular basis until the consumer bankrupt is discharged. This is called "surplus" income; in other words, income above and beyond what the bankrupt requires for living and expenses.

On bankruptcy, the trustee must apply the Superintendent's standards to the consumer bankrupt's income, and where there is surplus income according to the standards, the consumer bankrupt must pay that sum on a monthly basis until the bankrupt is discharged or until the court orders that payments stop. If the consumer bankrupt disagrees with the amount determined by the trustee, the consumer bankrupt may apply to the Official Receiver to mediate the amount of surplus income that should be paid to the trustee.

The amount generally corresponds to the provincial garnishment rules of approximately 20 to 30 percent of the gross salary having regard to the consumer bankrupt's family responsibilities and personal situation. In the case of after-acquired property, that is, property the consumer bankrupt acquires following the assignment and before discharge, the trustee in bankruptcy must intervene and take the property before the bankrupt can deal with it. In other words, the trustee must intercept payment to the bankrupt or seize the property if it remains in the consumer bankrupt's hands.

2. Property the Trustee Is Not Entitled to Take (Exemptions or Exclusions)

The provision dealing with a consumer bankrupt's property in the *Bankruptcy and Insolvency Act* also goes on to provide that the trustee in bankruptcy does not acquire or claim any right of property that is held in trust for another person or property that is exempt from seizure under the law of the province in which the bankrupt resides. The trustee is not entitled to the two following types of property.

2.1 Property held by the bankrupt for another

The trustee is not entitled to take property held by the bankrupt for another. If the bankrupt holds an investment fund in his or her name as a trustee for investors pursuant to an agreement, where the investors are friends and there are documents to support the transaction, then the trustee is not entitled to the fund. There must, however, be sufficient documents that support the trust claim and show that the property belongs to someone else.

In business bankruptcies, the federal government has specific rights under legislation to trace source deductions to the bankrupt's property which rank even ahead of the secured creditors. These source deductions cover income tax payments, Canada Pension payments, and employment insurance premiums. They are known as deemed trusts. Both of these are examples of trust property that do not go to the creditors, and therefore, the trustee in bankruptcy cannot make a claim to the property.

2.2 Property that is exempt from execution under the laws of the province or territory within which the property is located or within which the bankrupt resides

Generally, the consumer bankrupt can keep —

- ◆ insurance proceeds resulting from personal injuries arising, for example, from a motor vehicle accident;

- ◆ most, if not all, his or her salary, clothing, and household furniture, including wedding rings; and

- ◆ tools of the job or trade up to a prescribed amount in each province and territory.

In some provinces, there is a homestead exemption which permits the bankrupt to retain his or her home up to a certain amount of money.

In Ontario, for example, the consumer bankrupt can retain monies invested in a pension so long as the pension is registered under provincial legislation which exempts such monies from seizure. Other provinces have similar legislation. Similarly, if the consumer bankrupt has invested in a life-insured annuity or has an RRSP, the monies are protected from creditors and the trustee in bankruptcy under provincial life insurance legislation and under the *Bankruptcy and Insolvency Act*. However, if the debtor contributes to an RRSP within one year of bankruptcy, the trustee is entitled to seize the last contribution.

Once a consumer debtor is in bankruptcy, all creditors who have claims against the consumer bankrupt are prohibited from taking any remedy against the consumer bankrupt or against his or her property without the permission of the court. Secured creditors, like a mortgagee of real property such as a house, do not require permission but may continue to foreclose or exercise the power of sale remedy without interference by the trustee in bankruptcy. As long as the secured creditor does not claim anything against the estate, the secured creditor does not need court permission to commence or continue its enforcement.

3. Exempt Property

As the consumer bankrupt is entitled to keep exempt property, it is necessary to review the exemptions under federal law as well as in each of the provinces and territories. It is common for the trustee in bankruptcy to request that the consumer bankrupt complete an affidavit setting out his or her exempt property. In some cases where the exempt property may exceed the monetary exemptions, the trustee may engage an appraiser to value the assets being claimed as exempt. If the assets exceed the exemption, the trustee will require the consumer bankrupt to purchase the differential or the value in excess of the exemption.

There is clear need in every province and territory, first to coordinate what should be exempt and second, to determine higher limits so as to give the bankrupt some fairness in the present economic reality. The nature and size of exemptions varies from province to province. The following lists several exemptions for each province. The consumer debtor should consult local trustees in bankruptcy and local lawyers to determine the exemptions on taking bankruptcy protection.

The following sections discuss the exemptions federally and provincially.

3.1 Federal law

+ An annuity under the *Government Annuities Act*

+ Benefits under the *Canada Pension Plan Act*

+ Allowances under the *War Veteran Allowance Act*

+ Benefits under the *Old Age Security Act*

- Real and personal property of an Indian or a band situate on a reserve under the *Indian Act*
- Benefits under the *Employment Insurance Act*
- Benefits under the *Canadian Forces Superannuation Act*
- Pension funds under Registered Retirement Savings Plans (RRSPs) except for the contributions made within the year before bankruptcy

In all provinces and territories, there is *Wages Act* legislation that exempts an employee's wages or a variable amount from execution.

3.2 Alberta

The principal legislation dealing with exemptions is the *Civil Enforcement Act*. The following are some of the exemptions:

- Food required by the debtor and dependents
- Necessary clothing up to $4,000
- Medical and dental aids
- Household furnishings and appliances not exceeding $4,000
- Personal property used to earn income from an occupation not exceeding $10,000
- Vehicle not exceeding $5,000
- Property in registered plans, disability plans, and retirement plans
- The principal residence of an execution debtor not exceeding $40,000 of the debtor's equity
- If the debtor's source of living is farming, 160 acres of land on which the debtor's residence is located
- Personal property necessary for the proper conduct of farming operations
- Proceeds of life insurance where the beneficiary is a family member

3.3 British Columbia

The principal legislation dealing with exemptions is the *Court Order Enforcement Act*. The following are some of the exemptions:

- Necessary clothing of the debtor and dependents
- Household furnishings up to value of $4,000
- Medical and dental aids
- Tools up to a value of $10,000 used to earn income from the debtor's occupation
- Vehicle up to $5,000 in value
- Homestead exemption of $12,000 for the debtor's principal residence if it is located in the Capital Region District or Greater Vancouver; otherwise, the exemption is $9,000 if the residence is elsewhere in the province
- Property in RRIFs, RRSPs, and deferred profit-sharing plans
- Proceeds from life insurance where the beneficiary is a family member

3.4 Manitoba

The principal legislation dealing with exemptions are the *Judgments Act* and *Executions Act*. The following are some of the exemptions:

- Furniture and household furnishings and appliances not exceeding $4,500
- Necessary and ordinary clothing of the debtor and the members of his or her family
- Food and fuel necessary for the debtor and the members of his or her family for a period of six months, or the cash equivalent thereof
- Tools and implements used in the practice of a trade, occupation, profession, or business not exceeding $7,500
- Vehicle required for employment not exceeding $3,000
- Health aids
- If the debtor is a farmer, farm machinery, equipment, and a motor vehicle
- Exemptions cannot be claimed on behalf of the debtor who is about to remove himself or herself or abscond from the province

- Homestead exemption up to 160 acres if debtor and family actually reside on or cultivate the property
- Proceeds of life insurance where the beneficiary is a family member

3.5 New Brunswick

The principal legislation dealing with exemptions is the *Memorials and Executions Act*. The following are some of the exemptions:

- Furniture, household furnishings, and appliances used by the debtor and family
- Necessary ordinary wearing apparel for the debtor and family
- Tools, equipment, or chattels used in the debtor's occupation not exceeding $6,500
- Medical or health aids
- Proceeds of insurance where the beneficiary is a family member

3.6 Newfoundland and Labrador

The principal legislation dealing with exemptions is the *Judgment Enforcement Act*. The following are some of the exemptions:

- Food required by the debtor and his or her dependents during the 12 months after bankruptcy
- Necessary clothing of the debtor and his or her dependents that is of a value not exceeding $4,000
- Household furnishings, utensils, equipment, and appliances that are of a value not exceeding $4,000
- Vehicle of a value not exceeding $2,000
- Medical and dental aids
- The principal residence of a debtor that is of a value not exceeding $10,000
- Property in a registered plan including pensions, RRSPs, RRIFs, and DPSPs
- Any tools used by the debtor in the practice of the debtor's trade, profession, or occupation not exceeding $10,000

- Proceeds from life insurance where the beneficiary is a family member

3.7 Northwest Territories

The principal legislation dealing with exemptions is the *Exemptions Act*. The following are some of the exemptions:

- Household furnishings, utensils, equipment, and appliances needed by the debtor and any dependants

- Necessary and ordinary clothing of the debtor and any dependants

- Food, fuel, and other necessaries of life

- Tools, instruments, books, and personal property ordinarily used by the debtor in his or her business, profession, trade, or occupation

- An interest in the principal residence of the debtor, to the extent of that interest

- Medical and dental aids

- Vehicle

- Money payable under the *Social Assistance Act*

3.8 Nova Scotia

The principal legislation dealing with exemptions is the *Personal Property Security Act*. The following are some of the exemptions:

- Furniture, household furnishings, and appliances used by the debtor or a dependent to a realizable value of $5,000

- A vehicle having a realizable value of not more than $6,500 if the vehicle is required by the debtor in the course of the debtor's trade, profession, or occupation

- Medical or health aids

- Consumer goods in the possession and use of the debtor or a dependent

- Proceeds of insurance where the beneficiary is a family member

3.9 Nunavut

The principal legislation dealing with exemptions is the *Exemptions Act*. The following are some of the exemptions:

- Household furnishings, utensils, equipment, and appliances needed by the debtor and the family of the debtor to maintain a functional household

- Necessary and ordinary clothing of the debtor and the family of the debtor

- Food, fuel, and other necessaries of life required by the debtor and the family of the debtor for the 12 months following bankruptcy

- Tools, instruments, and other chattels ordinarily used by the debtor in his or her business, profession, or calling

- Tools, instruments, motor vehicles, all-terrain vehicles, snowmobiles, watercraft, and other chattels ordinarily used and needed by the debtor in hunting or fishing for food

- An interest in a house, a condominium, or an equivalent facility that is used by the debtor as his or her principal residence, to the extent of the interest, not exceeding the prescribed amount

- Medical and dental aids and devices

3.10 Ontario

Most of the exemptions are set out in the *Execution Act*. The province amends the Act infrequently as to the nature of the exemption and the amount. Exemptions do not include debts incurred with respect to purchase of beds, bedding, and wearing apparel, or homesteads.

- Necessary and ordinary wearing apparel of the debtor and his or her family not exceeding $5,650

- Household goods, food, and fuel not exceeding $11,300

- Tools, instruments, and other chattels ordinarily used by the debtor not exceeding $11,300

- In the case of a person engaged solely in tillage of soil or farming, livestock, foul, bees, tools, and implements up to $28,300

- In the case of a person engaged solely in the tillage of soil or farming sufficient seed to seed all his or her land up to 100 acres

- Vehicle up to a value of $5,650

- Eighty percent of wages are exempt from seizure or attachment subject to variation

- Proceeds of pension money where the pension is registered under the *Pension Act of Ontario*

- Proceeds of insurance where the beneficiary is a family member

3.11 Prince Edward Island

The principal legislation dealing with exemptions is the *Judgment and Execution Act*. The following are some of the exemptions:

- The necessary and ordinary clothing of the debtor and family

- Vehicle owned by the debtor not exceeding $3,000 in value

- The household furniture, utensils, equipment, food, and fuel that are contained in and form part of the permanent home of the debtor, not exceeding $2,000 in value

- In the case of a debtor other than a farmer, tools, instruments, and other chattels ordinarily used by the debtor in a business, trade, or calling, not exceeding $2,000 in value

- Farming exemptions including livestock and seed

- Proceeds from life insurance where the beneficiary is a family member

3.12 Quebec

The principal legislation dealing with exemptions is the *Code of Civil Procedure*. The following are some of the exemptions:

- The movable property which furnishes the debtor's main residence, used by and necessary for the life of the household, up to a market value of $6,000

- The food, fuel, linens, and clothing necessary for the life of the household

- The instruments of work needed for the personal exercise of the debtor's professional activity

- Consecrated vessels

- Family papers and portraits, medals, and other decorations

- Payments under support orders

- Benefits payable under a supplemental pension plan and disability insurance plans

- Salaries and wages up to 70 percent subject to variation

- Works of art and historical property

- Payments under an annuity

3.13 Saskatchewan

The principal legislation dealing with exemptions are *The Enforcement of Money Judgments Act* and *The Saskatchewan Farm Security Act*. The following are some of the exemptions:

- Clothing and jewellery with a cumulative value that does not exceed $7,500

- Medical and dental aids

- Household furnishings, utensils, equipment, and appliances

- Domestic animals that are kept solely as pets with a cumulative value that does not exceed $2,000

- Vehicle with a value that does not exceed $10,000

- Items of tangible personal property, other than a vehicle, required for use by the judgment debtor to earn income

- Seventy percent employment income subject to variation

- Interest in a home or house trailer not exceeding $50,000

- House and buildings occupied by the debtor not exceeding $32,000

- Where the debtor is a farmer, furniture and household furnishings and appliances not exceeding $10,000

- Proceeds from life insurance where the beneficiary is a family member

3.14 Yukon

The principal legislation dealing with exemptions is the *Exemptions Act*. The following are some of the exemptions:

- The household furniture, utensils, and equipment that are in the debtor's home

- A claim for clothing, food, fuel, or shelter supplied for the debtor or the debtor's family

- The necessary and ordinary wearing apparel of the debtor and the debtor's family

- The food, fuel, and other necessaries of life required by the debtor and the debtor's family for the 12 months following bankruptcy

- Livestock, fowl, bees, books, tools, and implements and other chattels necessary to and actually in use by the debtor in the debtor's business, profession, or calling to the extent of $600

- The house and buildings occupied by the debtor to the extent of $3,000

4. Salary

A large portion of the consumer bankrupt's salary is generally exempt from seizure or attachment by the trustee in bankruptcy. As under provincial law, the *Wages Act* in Ontario, a consumer debtor's salary can be attached or garnisheed to satisfy a debt to a creditor. In Ontario, for example, a creditor can seize up to 20 percent of the debtor's salary. The court has the discretion to grant a greater or lesser exemption having regard to the bankrupt's ability to make payment. In family law matters, a spouse can attach up to 50 percent of the debtor's salary.

There is a similar provision under the *Bankruptcy and Insolvency Act.* Following bankruptcy, the trustee in bankruptcy must request that the consumer bankrupt pay the estate surplus income from his or her salary or remuneration or commission while being undischarged. The determination of the amount to be paid usually follows the Superintendent's Standards. These standards are published annually from information received from Statistics Canada having regard to the bankrupt's station in life and family responsibilities. The Standards apply across Canada without any consideration as to the region or city. See Appendix III.

At the time of preparing the Assignment and the Statement of Affairs, the trustee in bankruptcy also reviews with the consumer bankrupt the income and expenses to determine what may be available to pay the estate. The consumer bankrupt has an obligation to produce an income and expense statement with proper back-up receipts, bills, and invoices. If the trustee and the consumer bankrupt cannot agree on the amount of the surplus income that should be contributed to the creditors, then the trustee can apply to the Official Receiver for mediation. If this fails, and the parties still cannot agree as to the amount of surplus income, either the trustee in bankruptcy or the consumer bankrupt may apply to the court for a determination.

If the bankrupt and the trustee cannot agree on the surplus income requirement, then the bankrupt can request the intervention of the Official Receiver to mediate the dispute. Similarly, any creditor who does not agree with the surplus income requirement can request the trustee to invoke the mediation procedure. The Official Receiver has the authority to resolve the dispute as to how much the bankrupt should pay the trustee. Unlike a judge or registrar, the mediator cannot fix the amount. The Official Receiver, as a mediator, reviews the bankrupt's income and expenses with a view to determining what the bankrupt can afford to pay his or her creditors. The mediator takes into account the bankrupt's personal and family situation. The mediator listens to the bankrupt's concerns and then listens to what the trustee has to say. To assist both parties, the mediator refers to the standards which contain statistics on the number of persons in the household, the net and gross incomes of each person, and then the expenses. While the mediator assists in having the bankrupt and the trustee come to some resolution, the mediator does not give legal advice and cannot make any binding declarations or orders.

If the bankrupt and the trustee agree with the mediator, then they will enter a mediation settlement agreement. If they are unable to agree, the trustee should apply to the court to determine the issue.

5. Property Conveyed Away

Under the *Bankruptcy and Insolvency Act*, the trustee in bankruptcy also has the right to recover any property of the consumer debtor that was wrongfully conveyed away to others prior to or during bankruptcy. This right arises in three different ways.

First, if the consumer debtor gives away his or her property to a friend or family member, or even to a stranger, without receiving any money or very little money in exchange for its value, then the trustee has the right to sue that person, called a transferee, for the return of the property. For example, if the consumer debtor transfers his interest in the matrimonial home to his wife for a nominal amount at a time when he was having difficulty in making payments to his creditors, then the trustee in bankruptcy can commence a lawsuit against the wife claiming an interest in the home for the creditors. In law, this is called a fraudulent conveyance or a transfer at undervalue. If the transfer takes place within one year of bankruptcy, then it is presumed that the transfer is void and will usually be set aside. However, if the transfer takes place outside the one-year period, then the trustee in bankruptcy must show the court that the consumer debtor, now bankrupt, needed the property at the time in order to pay his debts when he transferred the property to his wife. This is usually more difficult for the trustee to prove.

Second, if the consumer debtor pays any of his or her creditors or returns merchandise to them within three months of the date of bankruptcy, the trustee in bankruptcy can sue the creditor for the return of the payment or merchandise. However, the consumer debtor must be insolvent at the time of payment and have intended to prefer the particular creditor. So, if the consumer debtor pays one creditor when all other creditors are not being paid, the trustee can proceed to recover the payment. This is called a fraudulent preference. If the creditor is related to the consumer debtor, by blood or marriage, the three-month period is extended to one year. In other words, the trustee can sue that creditor if the payment is made within one year of bankruptcy.

Third, if the consumer debtor pays or transfers property to another where the value of the property is worth more than the payment, the trustee in bankruptcy has the right to recover the difference. For example, if the consumer debtor owes his or her accountant $1,000 for services and before bankruptcy, he or she gives the accountant a computer worth $3,000, the trustee can sue the accountant for the difference, or $2,000. This is called a transfer at undervalue. In this case, there is a one-year period before bankruptcy where the trustee can review all transactions entered into by the consumer debtor to see whether the consumer debtor received or gave fair value for the transfer of property.

Chapter 7
WHAT DEBTS SURVIVE BANKRUPTCY?

While the bankruptcy system is designed to relieve the honest, but unfortunate, debtor from his or her debts, it does not operate to wipe out everything. Once the consumer debtor has filed an assignment or has been placed into bankruptcy, most creditors who have claims against the consumer debtor are prevented from continuing their lawsuits or calling on the consumer debtor for payment. The general rule is that creditors are prevented from suing the consumer bankrupt once protection is taken under the *Bankruptcy and Insolvency Act*. Collection agencies cannot call on the consumer debtor demanding payment throughout the bankruptcy. On discharge, or getting out of bankruptcy, the consumer bankrupt's debts are wiped out or released. In this chapter, there is a review of the exceptions, or what debts survive or are not released on a consumer bankrupt's discharge.

On the consumer bankrupt's discharge, the bankrupt, now discharged, is released from most unsecured debts incurred prior to taking protection. The bankrupt is released from credit card debt, loans, mortgages, IOUs, bank loans, lines of credit, payday loans, and even income tax debts. If the bankrupt has mortgaged his or her home, only the unsecured portion is released. For example, the consumer debtor mortgaged his or her home for $200,000, and the mortgage company subsequently sells the home for $150,000, the consumer would be responsible for the shortfall, or $50,000 and that amount would be released on his or her discharge.

Debts incurred subsequent to taking protection are payable in full. The bankruptcy will not protect the consumer debtor for these debts. Other debts described below are not released.

I. Claims That Survive Bankruptcy

Bankruptcy is not a clearing house for all debts that the consumer debtor has incurred. Once the consumer debtor obtains an order of discharge, the order operates to release or discharge the consumer debtor from all claims provable in the bankruptcy except for certain types of claims. In other words, if the consumer debtor goes bankrupt, certain creditors can sue or continue their lawsuit against the consumer debtor as though the bankruptcy never happened. These types of claims are discussed in the following sections. These creditors have a choice as to when they want to sue:

♦ They can apply to the court while the consumer debtor is undischarged or still under bankruptcy protection and seek permission of the court to sue the consumer debtor.

♦ They can continue their lawsuit if they have already started one when the consumer debtor went bankrupt.

♦ They can wait until the consumer debtor gets out of bankruptcy or is discharged and then sue the consumer debtor.

In all other cases, the debts are released when the consumer bankrupt receives his or her discharge. In other words, the creditor is prohibited from suing on its debt, or technically, the debt is released. The following types of claims under the *Bankruptcy and Insolvency Act* are not released when the consumer debtor obtains a final discharge.

1.1 Fines and penalties

Court-imposed claims based on fines or penalties are not released when a consumer bankrupt gets discharged. For example, if the consumer debtor obtains a highway traffic fine, the *Bankruptcy and Insolvency Act* does not wipe out this debt. Similarly, if a court grants a restitution order in respect of a bankruptcy or criminal offence or any debt arising out of a recognizance or bail is not released on the discharge.

1.2 Alimony, maintenance, and support

If the consumer debtor is divorced, or married but separated, any debts or liabilities arising out of alimony or maintenance or as a result of a support order being made against one or the other spouse continue to be enforceable. Support orders include claims for spousal and child support and agreements between spouses whereby one spouse must pay the other. However, not all debts created under a separation agreement survive discharge. For example, an equalization payment under a separation agreement is not protected and therefore, the consumer debtor's obligation to pay is released on the spouse's discharge.

Often, a consumer debtor may go bankrupt thinking that he or she will be relieved from paying alimony, maintenance, or support orders. That is not the case. The support debtor, now bankrupt, must continue to make these payments. If the bankrupt fails to pay, these orders may be enforced through conventional remedies and special family law legislation even though the consumer debtor is in bankruptcy or subsequently discharged.

In addition to the support creditor's right to collect payments during and after the debtor's discharge, Parliament also gave the support creditor a preferred claim in the bankrupt estate. In 1997, the Parliament amended the *Bankruptcy and Insolvency Act* to provide that spousal and child support claims were provable as preferred claims for periodic amounts accrued during the year before bankruptcy and for any lump sum amounts. Further, support creditors may proceed to collect support claims during the bankruptcy including attaching or garnisheeing the bankrupt's salary.

1.3 Claims based on fraud and misrepresentation

Any debt arising out of fraud while acting in a fiduciary capacity, embezzlement, or misappropriation remains with the consumer debtor. This exception protects creditors who were defrauded by the bankrupt. When the consumer debtor goes bankrupt, such a debt does not disappear. The terms, "fraud," "embezzlement," or "misappropriation" relate primarily to convictions under the Canadian Criminal Code. Sometimes, it is possible for the court to make a certain type of order requiring the bankrupt to pay back the victim. This type of order is called a restitution order and is referred to in section **1.1**, fines and penalties. Bankruptcy discharge does not release this type of claim.

In addition, there is an exception for any debt for property obtained by fraudulent misrepresentation. This type of debt is more common in practice. Virtually all credit applications of a bank or a trust company that are filled out for a loan or for the issuance of a credit card contain a list of all the consumer debtor's assets and liabilities; that is, a list in chart form of what the consumer debtor owns and what the consumer debtor owes. On the application, there is a term whereby the consumer debtor lists all his or her assets and liabilities and a representation and acknowledgment that the bank or other lender is relying on the consumer debtor's proper completion of the statement in deciding on whether it will give the consumer debtor credit.

If the consumer debtor has made a material mistake, such as forgetting to identify a loan to another bank, listing assets that are not owned by the debtor, or grossly overstating his or her income, then it is possible that the bank may sue while the consumer debtor is in bankruptcy or once the consumer debtor gets discharged. If the court concludes that the consumer debtor's conduct was fraudulent, the consumer debtor will continue to be liable for the debt and bankruptcy will have been a waste of time. Such claims depend on the size of the debt. If the amounts are high enough to an institutional credit card holder, for example VISA or MasterCard, then that credit card holder may bring an action or continue an action that was started before the consumer debtor went bankrupt, or after the consumer debtor has been discharged for claims based on fraudulent misrepresentations on the applications for credit.

1.4 Claims based on student loans

Until 1997, there were no special provisions dealing with student loans. Technically, student loans were released on the bankrupt's discharge. However, courts from across the country often imposed payment terms on students as a condition of discharge. The courts considered the special purpose of the loans to students so that they could advance their education and provide for future greater earning capacity. As a result of the abuse, the Act was amended several times to provide that any debt or obligation arising out of a student loan, whether federal, provincial, or territorial will not be released for seven years from the date that the student ceases to be a full- or part-time student.

However, the bankrupt can apply to the court to vary the order if the bankrupt has or continues to experience financial difficulties and is acting in good faith in attempting to make payments.

1.5 Other claims that survive bankruptcy

There are other types of claims that survive discharge, but these do not come up in practice as readily. For example, a bankrupt is not discharged from payment of a damages award by a court in civil proceedings in respect to a claim based on bodily harm intentionally inflicted, a claim based on sexual assault, or one for wrongful death.

In addition, the consumer debtor remains liable for a dividend if a creditor's name was missed in the initial reporting stage and the creditor was never notified of the bankruptcy. If a consumer debtor's assets produce sufficient monies to pay creditors and a certain creditor did not know about it, then that creditor has a claim against the discharged bankrupt for failing to notify the trustee.

In practice, a creditor who has a claim that survives the discharge or that is not released on discharge will usually wait until the bankrupt is discharged and then may sue for the debt. Therefore, a consumer debtor should be careful in reviewing his or her liabilities with respect to the above exceptions if the consumer debtor considers making an Assignment.

Chapter 8
WHAT ARE THE BANKRUPT'S DUTIES?

It is important for the consumer debtor to know what is expected of him or her before going through the bankruptcy process, so this chapter reviews the duties of a consumer bankrupt. The consumer debtor should be familiar with and understand the proceedings so that there will be no surprises.

In most cases of consumer bankruptcies, there is seldom any risk of severe consequences if the consumer bankrupt does not comply with the duties, except perhaps on the consumer bankrupt's hearing for discharge if there is an opposition (which is a possibility if there is a disgruntled creditor, a creditor has a claim that survives discharge, or a trustee who has not been paid in full). While the bankrupt may be in breach of his or her duties, there are seldom any bankruptcy or criminal charges laid. However, if the bankrupt is non-cooperative or his or her conduct flagrantly abuses the duties, the trustee or Official Receiver will proceed to lay charges.

In such cases, the court may find the bankrupt guilty of an offence under the Act. In extreme cases, the bankrupt may face both a fine and imprisonment. And, the bankrupt can expect not to be discharged for some time. While undischarged, the bankrupt has no freedom to spend money, is not yet clear of the trustee and procedures, and must report his or her income on a regular basis and advise the trustee of any acquired assets. More about living as an undischarged bankrupt in Chapter 13.

There are many duties that are imposed on the bankrupt during the course of the administration. The consumer bankrupt is required to perform the following among other duties.

I. Deliver Property

The consumer bankrupt must advise and deliver all property that is under his or her control to the trustee including credit cards issued in the consumer bankrupt's name. The definition of property under his or her control is property that the consumer bankrupt has at the date of bankruptcy and property that the consumer bankrupt may acquire after bankruptcy, but before discharge. As indicated above, the consumer bankrupt must deliver all personal property that he or she has at the date of bankruptcy to the trustee that is not exempt under the laws of the province in which the consumer bankrupt resides or carries on business, or that is not held in trust by the consumer bankrupt for someone else. (More about exemptions in Chapter 6.)

In practice, the consumer bankrupt does not actually deliver all his or her personal property including clothing and household effects to the trustee. Rather, the consumer bankrupt completes an affidavit attesting to the exemptions; that is, the household effects are valued having regard to the exemptions afforded by federal and provincial law. The trustee seldom becomes involved in reviewing each piece of clothing, furnishing, and other personal possessions. However, if the creditors or inspectors instruct the trustee, the trustee can become engaged in a review of household items and have the exempt items valued by a liquidator.

As far as after-acquired property is concerned — that is, property acquired by the consumer bankrupt after filing an Assignment and before discharge — the trustee must request that the consumer bankrupt deliver it to the trustee.

In most cases, the consumer bankrupt's after-acquired property is the salary or wages that is earned from employment. In comparison, bankrupt corporations do not have after-acquired property. The trustee will want to attach or garnishee about 20 to 30 percent of the gross wages owing to the bankrupt, which must be paid into the estate, and ultimately the accumulated total will be paid to the creditors according to the priorities of secured creditors first, preferred creditors second, and then unsecured or ordinary creditors.

In addition to salary, the trustee has the right to seize an inheritance that may be left from a relative or from a friend, where that person dies while the consumer bankrupt is an undischarged bankrupt.

1.1 Make an inventory

As part of delivering property, the consumer bankrupt must make or assist the trustee in bankruptcy in making a list with respect to inventory of his or her assets, and complete some form of declaration or affidavit as to exempt items.

1.2 Deliver books

The consumer bankrupt must deliver books and records relating to his or her property including bank statements, credit card statements, life insurance policies, RRSPs, and RRIFs. (RESPs, however, in kids' names, are property of the kids in trust, and not the debtor.)

The trustee requires these documents in order to verify that the consumer bankrupt owns the assets and has properly insured them. The trustee will then be in a position to advise creditors if they ask questions about the consumer bankrupt's assets. The consumer bankrupt is also required to deliver tax records and tax returns to the trustee. Such records often reveal information that the consumer bankrupt forgot to advise or clarify a situation that had tax consequences.

If the trustee has reason to believe that the consumer bankrupt is hiding assets or is not disclosing everything, the trustee can intercept mail directed to the bankrupt on obtaining an order from the court. In addition, the trustee can examine the bankrupt under oath and the transcript of such examination can be used later against the bankrupt.

1.3 Submit a Statement of Affairs

The consumer bankrupt must, within five days of bankruptcy, prepare and submit a Statement of Affairs verified by affidavit showing the particulars of the assets and the liabilities, the names and the addresses of the creditors, and the particulars of any secured creditors. In consumer bankruptcies, this statement is prepared at the same time as the Assignment is drafted. The trustee requires the list of creditors so that the notice to creditors can be prepared advising of the bankruptcy and the right to call a meeting of creditors, as well as notify the creditor of the stay of proceedings against the bankrupt. The trustee needs this information as soon as possible as the trustee is under an obligation to notify creditors of the bankruptcy.

If the consumer is put into bankruptcy, the trustee must contact the consumer bankrupt immediately and request his or her attendance to prepare the Statement of Affairs.

2. Assist and Co-operate with the Trustee

The consumer bankrupt is required to co-operate with the trustee and perform any obligation required by the court, generally throughout the administration of the estate.

The *Bankruptcy and Insolvency Act* imposes a number of duties that the consumer bankrupt must perform including assisting the trustee in identifying assets and listing creditors. If the consumer bankrupt fails to perform these duties, then the trustee may apply for an order to compel the consumer bankrupt to perform them, or the consumer bankrupt can be fined up to $5,000, sent to jail, or both. In addition, the trustee must report the consumer bankrupt's conduct to the court if, as, and when there is an application for discharge. The court will take these breaches of duties into consideration in determining the outcome of the discharge hearing.

3. Disclose Property That Has Been Conveyed Away

The consumer bankrupt must inform the trustee in bankruptcy what property that the consumer bankrupt has disposed of, given away, or sold within the five years before the bankruptcy. The consumer bankrupt must also tell the trustee how and to whom the property was conveyed and what was paid for it. This information is necessary for the trustee in bankruptcy and the creditors so that they may evaluate whether to pursue the person who or corporation that received the property.

Consider this example: If the consumer debtor, before bankruptcy, sold his car worth $15,000 to his son for $7,000, then the trustee has a claim against the son for the difference, or $8,000. In this case, the consumer debtor gave away property worth $8,000 which could have been used to pay creditors. That is unfair to the creditors and the transaction is considered a fraudulent conveyance or transfer at undervalue. The creditors will instruct the trustee to demand that the son pay $8,000. If the son refuses, the trustee can proceed to sue the son. In addition, the trustee should also trace the disposition of the $7,000 that the son gave to the father. Last, when the consumer attends the discharge hearing, the trustee will report these facts to the court.

3.1 Disclose property that has been gifted

The consumer bankrupt must disclose all property that has been disposed of by gift without payment or valuable consideration within five years of bankruptcy. Under this duty, the trustee in bankruptcy reports to the creditors that they have the right to set aside the gift with the result that the property revests in the name of the consumer bankrupt. The trustee can then sell the property for the estate.

Consider this example: The bankrupt husband conveyed the interest in the matrimonial home to his spouse 11 months before taking bankruptcy protection for "$2 and natural love and affection." If the home is worth $80,000 after providing for mortgages and taxes, then the bankrupt conveyed an asset to his spouse for virtually nothing at a time when the $80,000 could have paid his debts. In this case, the trustee could sue the non-bankrupt spouse for at least $80,000 if the property has maintained its value. If the trustee has no money to do this, the trustee will report these findings to the creditors who may themselves have the right to pursue this asset and sue the non-bankrupt spouse.

4. Attend All Meetings of Creditors, Examinations, Counselling Sessions, and before the Official Receiver

The consumer bankrupt must attend the first meeting of creditors and submit to an examination, if requested by the creditors. While the creditors may ask questions relating to the bankrupt's affairs, the consumer bankrupt is not under oath in these meetings. If the trustee wishes to examine the consumer bankrupt under oath, the trustee will formally notify the consumer bankrupt of this appointment.

In most bankruptcies, there is only one meeting of creditors, and in many consumer bankruptcy cases, none at all.

The bankrupt must attend other meetings of creditors if they are held. In addition, the consumer bankrupt must attend the trustee's office if he or she is needed to explain the nature of the assets or related matters. The consumer bankrupt must attend, if requested, any examination about his or her assets and property.

The consumer bankrupt must attend before the Official Receiver, if requested, for an examination under oath with respect to his or her conduct, the causes of bankruptcy, and the disposition of property. In consumer bankruptcies, the Official Receiver has discretion as to whether to require the bankrupt to attend the examination. For example, where the consumer bankrupt has numerous credit cards and used one credit card to pay another, the trustee or credit card holders may request an examination.

Most of the questions of the Official Receiver relate to information requested by Statistics Canada about the bankruptcy process in a particular area both geographically and in industry. Some questions delve into areas where the consumer bankrupt gave away or sold property to family and friends for amounts that may be less than fair value. In addition, the creditors and the trustee may supply the Official Receiver with questions to be put to the consumer bankrupt.

4.1 Attend counselling sessions

The consumer bankrupt must attend two counselling sessions during the bankruptcy. They are designed to assist consumer debtors in the management of funds and make the bankrupt aware of the financial problems. If the consumer bankrupt fails to attend, he or she will lose the right to be discharged automatically after nine months. The trustee or a qualified counsellor conducts the first counselling session within 60 days from the date of filing. The second counselling session is conducted within 210 days from the date of filing.

5. Perform Other Duties

There are other duties required of a bankrupt person as described in the following sections.

5.1 Aid in realization

The consumer bankrupt must assist the trustee in bankruptcy in selling or realizing on the assets. Depending on the nature and type of assets, the trustee may require the consumer bankrupt's information, input, and assistance.

5.2 Execute other documents

The consumer bankrupt must execute deeds, transfers, powers of attorney, and other documents when reasonably requested to by the trustee in bankruptcy. Sometimes, a purchaser may want assurances about certain assets, and in this case the trustee may request, for example, that the consumer bankrupt complete a statutory declaration as to the former ownership.

5.3 Examine proofs of claim and disclose false claims

The consumer bankrupt must examine the correctness of all proofs of claim filed with the trustee. The trustee may want to review the proofs with the consumer bankrupt to determine their completeness and accuracy. He or she must advise the trustee in bankruptcy of false claims that may have been filed.

5.4 Inform of any material change

The consumer bankrupt must inform the trustee in bankruptcy of any material change in his or her financial situation during bankruptcy.

5.5 Advise of change of address

The consumer bankrupt must keep the trustee advised of his or her address at all times before discharge.

Chapter 9
WHAT ARE THE ALTERNATIVES TO BANKRUPTCY?

In this chapter, there is a discussion about debtors who do not want to go bankrupt for a variety of reasons. Some debtors have a sense of pride and may wish to pay their creditors in full or otherwise make some form of compromise payment. Other debtors may enter into settlements with some creditors for part of the debt. Some people may frown upon bankruptcy as the ultimate financial failure, while creditors may withhold credit until the debtor has made satisfactory arrangements to pay the debts. There are other solutions to financial difficulties rather than going bankrupt. This chapter covers those other solutions. However, the decision to file for bankruptcy or to pursue other remedies is dependent on the unique circumstances of each individual.

Following are some alternatives to bankruptcy that may be considered.

1. Pay Something and Not Go Bankrupt

While it is only necessary to have debts in excess of $1,000 in order to meet one of the qualifications to go bankrupt, most consumer debtors have about ten creditors, mostly credit card companies, and many small businesses have far more than that. Where an individual person has few creditors, and the amount of debts to his or her creditors do not add up to a large amount of money, say $20,000, then it is possible to make settlements for payments less than the total amount owing without the formality of going into bankruptcy. This may take time and direct negotiations with the creditor. Often, the creditor may proceed to obtain a judgment and then attempt to enforce the judgment against the consumer debtor's assets. Only when the creditor finds out that there is not much to seize in satisfaction of the debt will the creditor be amenable to a method of repaying all or part of the debt. In cases where the consumer debtor has a job, the creditor will attempt to attach his or her wages.

Therefore, some consumer debtors will attempt to use their best efforts to stay out of bankruptcy by making arrangements directly or indirectly with their creditors while other consumer debtors may simply abandon their assets and property.

2. Seek Credit Counselling Assistance

In Ontario and in other provinces and territories, there are non-profit and for-profit credit counselling services. These credit counselling services serve to advise individuals who have personal money management problems and attempt to rearrange consumer debt through programs with consumer creditors.

In Ontario, the Ministry of Community and Social Services provides funding for credit counselling services in Ontario and the balance of funding is provided through such charities as United Way, local grants, and financing from credit granting companies.

The Ontario Association of Credit Counselling Services has offices throughout Ontario. Its website is www.oaccs.com. Many of the offices are in the Greater Toronto Area. It has a toll-free telephone number: 1-888-746-3328. Credit Counselling Service has many offices in Canada.

Credit counselling services may also be found using search engines or in the Yellow Pages under Credit Counselling Services or through community centre offices. There are other organizations that provide debt counselling. For example:

- Canadian Association of Debt Assistance: www.canadian associationofdebtassistance.org

- Credit Canada Debt Solutions: www.creditcanada.com or 1-800-267-2272

- Credit Counselling Canada: www.creditcounsellingcanada.ca or 1-866-398-5999

A credit counsellor interviews the individual debtor or family on a personal basis and obtains information about the individual's financial situation. The counsellor then analyzes the alternatives available and determines whether or not there are any available funds which could be paid to the creditors. At the same time, the counsellor advises the debtor as to preparing budgets and gives advice on using consumer credit cards. Ultimately, the credit counsellor attempts to arrange through the agency a repayment of creditors on a pro-rata system.

While such a payment does not have the force of law, many consumer creditors go along with that type of repayment as it eventually benefits each of the creditors and the debtor. If the creditors do not go along with this type of repayment, their ultimate remedy from the creditors' point of view is to sue or even put the debtor into bankruptcy. Usually, placing the debtor into bankruptcy results in no one receiving any further payment. Depending upon the amounts involved, if the debtor makes regular payments, albeit small, creditors often waive any past interest on the account. With interest rates at 18 to 40 percent on past due accounts, and even higher rates in recent years, the consumer debtor can be released of significant amounts of debt. For consumer debts that are less than $25,000, this is the best alternative short of filing a consumer proposal.

3. Deal with Creditors: An Informal Proposal

Where there are few creditors, it is sometimes possible for the consumer debtor to meet with his or her creditors and attempt to restructure payment. Sometimes, the consumer debtor may even suggest a compromise or offer a sum less than the full sum that is owing to the creditors. If the consumer debtor is honest and forthright and can show his or her income and available assets for realization and distribution, then creditors will often go along with the deal. In practice, this is called an informal proposal. An informal proposal does not have the force of law, but it is a workable arrangement if all the creditors do join in and agree to accept a form of repayment over time or something less than the full amount that is outstanding.

If there are many creditors, this method usually does not work as any one creditor can take legal proceedings to recover payments on its account. Attempting to enter an informal proposal with some creditors usually ends up in frustration, loss of much time and expense, and continued legal proceedings with no material results.

4. Apply for the Orderly Payment of Debts

Part X of the *Bankruptcy and Insolvency Act* sets up a system for the orderly payment of debts even though the consumer debtor is not bankrupt. This procedure is optional to each province as to whether this part applies as it is funded by the province under which it operates. The provinces of Alberta, British Columbia, Manitoba, Nova Scotia, Prince Edward Island, and Saskatchewan have all elected to have this part applied. Under Part X of the Act, a consumer debtor can apply to the clerk of the court for an order directing a method of paying the debts. Once the order is issued, the creditors are prevented from taking proceedings against the consumer debtor as long as the consumer debtor complies with the terms of the order. The consumer debtor may pay his or her debts over a three-year period without creditor harassment and wage assignments.

5. Make a Formal Proposal

Under the *Bankruptcy and Insolvency Act*, a consumer debtor may make a proposal to creditors. In 1992, Parliament amended the Act to provide new rules for a consumer proposal. If the proposal is made pursuant to Division II of Part III of the *Bankruptcy and Insolvency Act*, the proposal is protected by the terms of the Act and, more particularly, creditors cannot take legal proceedings against the consumer debtor until the administrator is discharged. The proposal is filed with a licensed trustee in bankruptcy together with a Statement of Affairs, that is, a Statement of Assets and Liabilities.

The proposal is put to the creditors on a vote called for that purpose and if a majority of creditors accept the proposal, then it proceeds through court approval. The effect of an order approving the proposal is that the proposal binds all creditors who dissented; in other words, those creditors who vote against the proposal are forced to take the offer of settlement if it is approved by the creditors and the court under the formula.

If the creditors reject the proposal, the consumer debtor is not automatically bankrupt, as a debtor would be if the debtor were a businessperson.

The court must determine whether the terms of the proposal are fair and reasonable, even though the creditors have already approved it. The court has the overriding function to protect the creditors from frivolous offers of settlement. Any one creditor who voted against the proposal may object at the court hearing. The terms of the proposal can vary from an offer extending the time to pay the debts to an offer making a compromise or a payment less than 100 cents on the dollar to the creditors. The terms of such proposals can vary with the imagination of the draftsperson. For consumers, a proposal may provide that the debtor pay a monthly sum to the trustee for a period of time, say three years, and after this occurs, the consumer debtor becomes released. The consumer proposal must be performed within five years.

Chapter 10 sets out in more detail the procedures for a consumer proposal.

Chapter 10
HOW DOES THE DEBTOR MAKE A CONSUMER PROPOSAL?

In this book, there is a review of the two types of proposals, the formal consumer proposal and the small-business debtor proposal (which is an option for consumers to use in some cases); this chapter covers the former. For more on small-business proposals, see Chapter 11.

Every attempt should be made to save the debtor from simply filing an assignment into bankruptcy, and a proposal is a good option to help avoid bankruptcy. If the debtor, whether consumer or small-business debtor, approaches creditors in a timely manner, it is likely that the debtor can stave off bankruptcy by making some form of compromise. Many small-business debtors can qualify as a consumer debtor. As a small-business debtor, the debtor can take advantage of the summary provisions under the Act. While the summary provisions favour lower costs to the trustee, the debtor benefits with the admission that there are no or very few assets to administer (which avoids the expense of a full administration, among other benefits). This in itself tells creditors that there is nothing to chase.

If the debtor makes a last-minute attempt to make a proposal that has no merit, the creditors will not likely have any sympathy for the debtor and a bankruptcy will eventually occur. The rules are slightly different for the two types of proposals.

I. Decide to Make a Consumer Proposal

Under the *Bankruptcy and Insolvency Act,* Division II of Part III permits an insolvent person to file a consumer proposal with a trustee in bankruptcy or an administrator to compromise his or her debts. The 1992 amendments to the Act permit an individual person, the consumer debtor, to make a proposal and avoid the stigma of bankruptcy. The 1997 amendments extend Division II to consumer bankrupts as well as in the proper circumstances, two or more individuals, such as a husband and wife, may file a joint consumer proposal. As a result, a husband and wife, who in most cases have the same creditors, may file a joint consumer proposal to their creditors. The 1997 amendments to the Act also streamline the procedures that are involved in the proposal process and attempt to reduce the costs of administration.

The provisions are designed to encourage consumers to make a proposal to their creditors rather than simply filing an assignment into bankruptcy.

An administrator is a licensed trustee or a person to be appointed or designated by the Superintendent of Bankruptcy to administer consumer proposals. The introduction of an administrator gives the Department of Industry Canada the flexibility to enlist credit counselling agencies as administrators to assist in the administration, provide bankruptcy services in remote areas where there are no licensed trustees, and gives the Department the opportunity to participate in the marketplace with the private sector.

A "consumer debtor" is defined in the Act to mean an insolvent person whose aggregate debts do not exceed $250,000 excluding the debts secured by the debtor's principal residence. However, the type of debts is not defined, with the result that a debtor having business debts may also qualify as a consumer debtor. The proposal must provide that the terms be performed within five years and that certain claims be paid in priority together.

In 2012, there were 122,751 bankruptcies and proposals in Canada. Of this number, 118,398 represented consumers. In turn, 71,495 filed for bankruptcy protection, while 46,903 made consumer proposals. On the business side, there were 3,236 business bankruptcies and 1,117 proposals, for a total of 4,353.

In 2012, Ontario, for example, had 48,742 bankruptcies and 24,278 proposals for a total of 73,020 cases.

As indicated earlier, a consumer debtor is an insolvent person whose aggregate debts do not exceed $250,000 excluding the debts secured by the debtor's principal residence. In other words, the consumer debtor must not have debts of more than $250,000, and in calculating the total debt, the debtor cannot add in the debt that may be owed on a mortgage of his or her home.

In consulting with a trustee, the debtor should review the best alternative to his or her financial problems. In many cases, the debtor will be able to make a consumer proposal which the creditors will accept. Readers can review the forms available in the download kit that comes with this book.

2. Cause an Investigation

Once the consumer decides to make a consumer proposal, and sees a licensed trustee or administrator, the administrator must investigate the consumer debtor's property and financial affairs so as to be able to assess the financial situation and the cause or causes of insolvency, provide financial counselling to the debtor, and prepare and file a proposal with the Official Receiver. The administrator reviews different types of proposals with the consumer debtor and chooses one that will be appropriate in the circumstances. In most cases, the consumer proposal provides that the debtor pay a weekly or monthly sum out of his or her earnings to the administrator for distribution to the creditors.

With the assistance of the administrator, the consumer debtor prepares a Statement of Affairs and a Statement of Income and Expenses which determines whether, and to what extent, the consumer debtor has surplus income which the debtor can pay on a monthly basis over a period of time but not exceeding five years. While the Act prescribes payment to certain creditors in priority to others, the consumer debtor need not be concerned as those payments are normally made from the accumulated monthly payments.

Once the administrator has reviewed the financial affairs, the administrator is then in a position to prepare a consumer debtor proposal. In the proposal, the consumer debtor must set out —

♦ terms that will be performed within five years,

- certain claims which will be paid in priority, and

- payment of all fees and expenses of the administrator arising out of the proposal and in respect of the counselling services to the debtor.

3. File the Documents

After the administrator files the proposal with the Official Receiver, the administrator must prepare within ten days of filing —

- a report as to the administrator's investigations;

- an opinion as to whether the proposal is reasonable and fair;

- a condensed statement of the consumer debtor's assets, liabilities, income, and expenses; and

- a list of creditors of more than $250.

Consumers can fill out the necessary forms themselves, but it won't save them any money. What it will help do is speed up the process overall, and give the debtor a better understanding of all proceedings. Once the consumer proposal has been filed, there is a stay of proceedings against all creditors of the consumer debtor, namely creditors are prohibited from taking any steps to sue or collect on any judgment. If the consumer debtor has given a wage assignment to secure a loan or his or her wages are being attached, the employer does not have any obligation to make deductions from the consumer debtor's wages to pay the administrator.

Within ten days of filing the consumer proposal with the Official Receiver, the administrator must then send the following documents to creditors:

- Copy of the proposal

- Copy of the report

- Proof of claim

- Statement to the effect that no meeting will be called unless one is requested

Ordinarily in corporate and commercial proposals, there is a meeting of creditors to discuss the merits of a proposal. However, in consumer proposals, there is not likely to be a meeting of creditors to consider the affairs of the bankrupt, to affirm the appointment of the administrator, and to give the administrator directions. So that the administration works more efficiently, there is no requirement to call a meeting of creditors unless the Official Receiver requests a meeting of creditors or if the creditors having at least 25 percent of the proven claims request a meeting.

If no one opposes the consumer proposal, or if no meeting of creditors is required, the consumer proposal is deemed to be accepted 45 days after its filing. If a meeting is held, a simple majority of creditors by ordinary resolution will carry the vote. If no creditor shows up at the meeting, the proposal will be deemed to have been accepted. Alternatively, the creditors can adjourn the meeting to permit an examination of the debtor before voting. Unless the Official Receiver or any other interested person requests a court hearing, the proposal is automatically deemed to have been approved by the court after the expiration of 15 days from the acceptance or deemed acceptance of the creditors. If a court hearing is requested, usually rare, the administrator will send notice to all creditors. The process then can be automatic without a meeting of creditors or a court application to approve the consumer proposal. Consequently, the administration of a consumer proposal is efficient and less expensive than the non-consumer debtor and small-business debtor.

Once the consumer proposal has been accepted by the creditors and automatically approved by the court, the debtor must perform the terms if he or she is to be released from paying the balance of the debts. While the consumer proposal is operative, no creditor can accelerate payment under a contract. This includes, for example, a vehicle lease payment or a lump sum payment under a mortgage and public utilities cannot terminate their supply of services.

The consumer proposal may be annulled by the court on several grounds. The first ground is the situation where the debtor defaults in the performance of any provision. If the debtor defaults in payments or if the proposal cannot continue without extraordinary delay, the court may set aside the consumer proposal. For example, if the debtor cannot maintain payments on a regular basis, the trustee or creditors may seek to annul the proposal. Second, the court may annul the proposal if the debtor was not eligible to qualify under this Division when it was filed. Third, if the proposal cannot continue without injustice or undue delay, the court may annul the proposal. Fourth, the court can annul the proposal if its court approval was obtained by fraud. Fifth, if the consumer debtor defaults in payment of more than three months in cases where there are monthly payments due, or other frequent payments, the consumer proposal will be deemed automatically to be annulled.

Unless otherwise ordered, where a consumer proposal is annulled, or deemed to be annulled, the consumer debtor is prohibited from making another proposal. If the consumer proposal is annulled, the administrator shall file a report with the Official Receiver and send a notice to the creditors informing them of the deemed annulment. Creditors can pursue or can continue pursing the debtor for payment. If the consumer proposal is made by a bankrupt and is subsequently annulled, the consumer debtor is deemed to have made an assignment into bankruptcy and the administrator is then required to call a meeting of creditors. In other cases where the court does not annul the proposal, the consumer debtor is prohibited from making another consumer proposal without a court order, and is not entitled the protection against seizing creditors. In other words, creditors may enforce their claims as though the proposal had not been filed.

Chapter 11
SMALL-BUSINESS PROPOSAL

While this book is primarily devoted to consumer insolvency and bankruptcy proceedings, this chapter offers a short comparison with a consumer proposal.

If the consumer debtor does not qualify under Division II for a consumer proposal, essentially, if the consumer has debts over $250,000 excluding any mortgage on the debtor's residence, the debtor can attempt to make an informal proposal with his or her creditors without taking bankruptcy protection, or the debtor can make a small-business proposal.

While an informal proposal or "work-out" does not have the force of law, it is feasible where the creditors all agree on the restructuring. The debtor has to decide (with professional advice) whether the "business" is worth saving. If it is not, then the debtor is best to close up and file an assignment into bankruptcy. Creditors generally will not accept a business proposal unless they can expect something more by way of a dividend and perhaps future revenue than if the business were to go bankrupt.

1. Decide to Make a Small-Business Proposal

In many cases, the small-business debtor will not have up-to-date financial information so that a proper assessment can be made. At the same time, creditors are pressing for payment of their accounts, and perhaps have commenced legal proceedings. If the small-business debtor does not have sufficient time to prepare a business proposal, the debtor will file a notice of intention to make a proposal along with a trustee's consent and a list of creditors over $250 with the Official Receiver in the district where the debtor carries on business. The trustee files these forms with the Official Receiver. The notice of intention operates to stay all legal proceedings against the debtor for a period up to 30 days. Within ten days of filing the Notice of Intention, the debtor must file a cash-flow statement and a report on the reasonableness of the cash-flow statement. The proposal trustee usually helps in the preparation of these documents.

If the small-business debtor has time to prepare the documents, then the debtor should do so as a reality check and for his or her own understanding of the situation, though the trustee will prepare the documents for filing. The trustee can file the proposal to the creditors, cash-flow statement, and Section 170 Report all at the same time.

As a result, the debtor has up to 30 days to file the proposal with the Official Receiver after the filing of the Notice of Intention (although technically the trustee will do the preparing and filing of the forms). If the debtor fails to file the cash-flow statement within the 10-day period, or fails to file the proposal within the 30-day period or during any extended period if granted by the court, then there is a deemed assignment in bankruptcy. This means that instead of using the proposal route, the debtor is automatically bankrupt.

When these documents are filed with the Official Receiver, all creditors including secured creditors cannot proceed to collect on their accounts.

The trustee under the proposal must monitor the debtor's financial situation and if the trustee finds a material adverse change, the trustee must report this to the court.

If the debtor cannot file a proposal within the first 30-day period, the debtor can apply to the court for an extension. The debtor can obtain several extensions up to a maximum of six months from the start if the debtor can show the court that he or she is acting in good faith and that the creditors are not "material prejudiced" (a legal term describing whether or not creditors are paid fairly). There is no provision to extend the time beyond the six months.

1.1 Types of proposals

Apart from the statutory requirements in a proposal, there is no prescribed formula or form for a proposal. The debtor must provide for the priority of preferred creditors, payment of current source deductions, and payment of GST/HST while the proposal is operative. Insofar as the type of proposal a debtor can make is concerned, the following scenarios are representative:

- Extension of time: the debtor may propose that the debts be paid over a period of time on a 100 percent (or less) basis.

- Composition of debts: the debtor may propose to pay a lump sum or a percentage on the dollar of the claims to the trustee for distribution to the creditors.

- A combination of an extension of time and composition.

- A basket proposal where the debtor conveys all, most, or some of its assets to a trustee for realization and distribution.

- A liquidation proposal whereby the debtor's assets are realized in an orderly manner rather than in a quick bankruptcy sale.

There are several advantages to both the debtor and the creditors if a proposal is accepted by the creditors and approved by the court. From the debtor's perspective —

- the debtor remains in business,

- principals of the debtor may be able to compromise statutory tax liabilities, and

- jobs are saved.

From the creditors' perspective —

- creditors receive a higher dividend than they would otherwise receive in a bankruptcy, and

- creditors can continue dealing with the debtor at their option.

2. Cause an Investigation

On the filing of a Notice of Intention or on the filing of the proposal itself, there is a stay of proceedings with respect to the rights and remedies of all creditors for 30 days, which may be extended by

45-day periods. Often, a debtor is not able to formulate a proposal within the initial 30-day period where creditors are pressing for payment or are threatening to enforce their security. The Notice of Intention gives the debtor a minimum 30 days to file a proposal while, at the same time, it stays the rights of creditors to continue or commence proceedings against the debtor. In addition, the stay operates to prevent anyone who is a party to an agreement with the insolvent person from terminating or amending the agreement or accelerating any payment by reason only of the filing and in the cases of leases and licensing agreements even though there are arrears in payments.

To protect creditors during the stay period, a trustee must become involved. The trustee is required to advise and assist the debtor in the preparation of the proposal during the period between the filing of the Notice of Intention and the filing of a proposal. During this time, and subsequently, the trustee can investigate the financial affairs and with some guidance, assist the debtor in making a proposal. The trustee must examine the debtor's property, books, records, and other financial information until the court approves the proposal or the insolvent person becomes bankrupt. The trustee must also file a report on the state of the insolvent person's business and to note any material adverse change in the projected cash-flow statement or the financial circumstances. Ultimately, the trustee must report and make recommendations on the proposal.

If the debtor requires financing during the proposal process, the debtor has to apply to the court for an order. Usually, secured creditors will want to know whether their interest in the debtor's property is protected. Secured creditors relying on the debtor's assets in advancing money are directly affected and are not likely to be aware of their position until after the order is made.

In acting for the creditors, the trustee must —

♦ appraise and investigate the affairs and property of the debtor;

♦ assure that the information in the cash-flow statement and report is reasonably accurate;

♦ deliver on request the cash-flow statement to any creditor;

♦ report to the creditors any material adverse change in the statement or financial circumstances;

♦ monitor the debtor's business and financial affairs. This means that the trustee shall have access to and examine the debtor's property, including its premises, books, records, and other financial documents, to the extent necessary to assess the debtor's business and financial affairs adequately; and

- report to the creditors in the prescribed form about the debtor's affairs.

3. Vote

Whereas in a consumer bankruptcy the meeting of creditors may not be necessary, in a business situation the trustee must call a meeting of creditors, which is to be held 21 days after the filing of the proposal. The trustee sends a notice to every known creditor, a condensed statement of assets and liabilities, a list of creditors, the proposal, and a proof of claim with a proxy.

Most trustees also send a report to the creditors outlining the history of the debtor, the causes of its insolvency, the terms of the proposal, a description of the documents, the proof of claim, the voting letter, and the trustee's recommendation. As the trustee is required under the Act to assist the debtor in drafting the proposal, the trustee invariably recommends its acceptance essentially on the basis that the creditors will receive a higher dividend on their claim than if the debtor were in bankruptcy. If the creditors reject the proposal, there is an automatic bankruptcy.

The Official Receiver or his or her delegate acts as chair. Usually, that is the trustee under the proposal.

Unsecured and secured creditors having proven claims may vote. Unsecured creditors can vote in one class unless otherwise provided in the proposal. Secured creditors may be included in more than one class. In voting on the proposal, each of the classes of unsecured and secured creditors must have a majority in number and at least two-thirds in value for the proposal to succeed. If the proposal is accepted by the creditors and approved by the court, it binds all unsecured claims and those secured claims that were affected by the terms. If the creditors do not accept the proposal, there is a deemed assignment in bankruptcy; if the court refuses to approve the proposal even though the creditors approved the proposal, there is also a deemed assignment.

In making the recommendation, the trustee has a conflict of interest since the trustee advocates the acceptance of the proposal by the creditors. If the trustee cannot recommend the acceptance of the proposal, it should not take the engagement, but recommend an assignment to the debtor. However, in most cases, the trustee will have reviewed the debtor's records in coming to that conclusion. If the debtor wishes to proceed with the proposal, the trustee will have a conflict of interest with the debtor. In that case, the debtor should pursue a substitute trustee to carry on.

If the creditors vote in favour of the proposal or as amended, the trustee applies to the court for an order setting the date of the hearing at which time the court will either ratify or will reject the proposal.

The court takes several interests into account when considering whether to approve the proposal and wants to —

- give the debtor an opportunity to meet and settle with the creditors without going into bankruptcy;
- protect the creditors generally by ensuring that what is offered to the creditors is reasonable, that there is some security in place to protect creditors, and by knowing that a majority of creditors has already approved it; and
- protect the public at large in the integrity of the bankruptcy legislation.

The court must satisfy itself that the —

- terms are reasonable;
- terms are calculated to benefit the general body of creditors; namely, that the creditors will receive a higher dividend than if the debtor were bankrupt;
- statutory terms have been complied with; and
- debtor has acted in good faith throughout.

If the trustee recommends the proposal and the creditors vote in favour of it, the court will not likely substitute its judgment unless there are compelling reasons put forth by objecting creditors.

If the court refuses to approve the proposal, the debtor is automatically in bankruptcy and the court can replace the trustee if it is satisfied that the replacement is in the best interests of the creditors.

Chapter 12
BANKRUPTCY AND INITIAL DOCUMENTS: AN OVERVIEW

This chapter reviews the mechanics of going bankrupt and what is expected of the consumer debtor from filing the assignment to discharge, and reviews the documents that are required.

Reminder: The consumer debtor should first consider whether a lawyer is needed. A bankruptcy or an insolvency lawyer can review the consumer debtor's financial affairs quickly and can advise whether there are any problems in proceeding with the bankruptcy. An accountant may be able to advise how to take advantage of any tax losses by suggesting a proposal to creditors rather than bankruptcy.

Also, the forms and documents shown in this book and in the download kit are examples included for readers' understanding and reference. A trustee or lawyer will assist with filling out and filing these forms.

1. Does the Consumer Debtor Need a Lawyer?

Once the consumer debtor becomes aware that he or she is having financial difficulties in meeting expenses and is psychologically ready to go bankrupt, he or she should seek the support of a family member or friend as to whether the services of a lawyer are needed. After bankruptcy, it is most difficult to reverse the proceedings if the consumer debtor subsequently decides that it was a mistake to file the assignment in bankruptcy.

This may sound repetitive, but it is important. The consumer debtor should see a lawyer first if he or she is not sure of his or her rights and obligations under contracts, the types of property that are exempt if there is a bankruptcy, and the type of property that becomes the property of the trustee. A lawyer will review the types of property that the consumer debtor owned over the last several years to see whether the trustee or creditors will be able to reclaim transfers of property made to family members and friends. The lawyer should ask many questions about the circumstances surrounding the transferring property, and generally relating to the consumer debtor's assets and liabilities.

In turn, the consumer debtor should be prepared and have a list of questions ready for the lawyer.

If the consumer debtor has a partner or spouse and both are insolvent to the same or similar creditors, then they can take protection as a couple under the *Bankruptcy and Insolvency Act*. In other words, both parties may assign themselves into bankruptcy using the same trustee. However, if they have separate creditors, they will not be able to take advantage of the joint filings. Before taking that step, it may be worthwhile to see a lawyer.

In choosing a lawyer, the consumer debtor should, where possible, rely on a friend or family member for suggestions. It is generally prudent to choose a lawyer who has bankruptcy and insolvency expertise. Such a person will be able to focus on the issues more readily and perhaps be less expensive than a general practitioner. As a starting place, the consumer should consult the Internet for a lawyer in the area he or she lives.

In Ontario, for example, there is an unofficial group of lawyers who are members of the Insolvency Section of the Ontario Bar Association, who specialize in bankruptcy matters. These persons are located throughout the province. It is also possible to find insolvency practitioners through the provincial and territorial sections of the Canadian Bar Association and on their websites. However, a general practitioner may be all that is required in this situation. If in doubt, the consumer debtor may request the general practitioner refer the matter to a specialist.

If the consumer has seen a lawyer, or if the consumer has decided that one is not necessary, he or she should make an appointment to see a trustee in bankruptcy. As indicated earlier, the consumer may find a trustee on the Internet, in the Yellow Pages of the telephone book, or as recommended by a lawyer, an accountant, or a friend.

2. Trustees: Costs and Paperwork

Usually on the initial visit, the trustee in bankruptcy gives the consumer debtor the first counselling session. The trustee reviews the consumer debtor's financial affairs, and particularly, the consumer debtor's income and expenses over a monthly period. After assembling this information, the trustee decides whether bankruptcy is the proper solution to the consumer debtor's financial problems. The trustee has a duty to review all options with the consumer. This visit usually takes about one hour if the consumer debtor has all the paperwork in order. Some trustees do not charge for the first consultation. The trustee will want to see —

- a list of all the consumer's creditors, their names, addresses, and amounts, together with back-up invoices and bills;
- a list of all the consumer's assets with information about each;
- details about assets that have been transferred or disposed of within the last five years; and
- information in order to prepare a detailed monthly budget.

If the consumer debtor comes prepared, the trustee can process the assignment, Statement of Affairs, and questionnaire more quickly.

The costs of making an assignment vary with the business practices of most trustees. However, the individual consumer debtor can expect to pay about $1,800. Sometimes, the consumer debtor has the money to pay the trustee; other times, the trustee may require a family member or a close friend to guarantee to pay the fees if the consumer does not have sufficient assets to cover them. In some cases, a trustee may take the assignment on a payment plan so long as the full fees are paid before the expiry of the nine-month period of bankruptcy for first-time bankrupts.

In a husband and wife bankruptcy, the costs may be something less than double. If the consumer debtor fails to pay, the trustee will oppose the discharge in which case there will be a hearing before the registrar or judge. At the discharge hearing, the court will decide whether the consumer shall pay additional monies as a condition of being discharged.

3. What Documents Does the Consumer Debtor Have to Sign?

Once the consumer debtor decides to file an Assignment into bankruptcy, the trustee sets up a second meeting soon after the first for the purpose of executing the bankruptcy papers.

The individual will complete the following:

♦ Assignment

♦ Statement of Affairs

♦ Appendices containing pertinent information relating to the affairs of the bankrupt

♦ Affidavit in support of exempt assets

♦ Commitment to paying fees and disbursements

The following sections describe the Assignment, and the Statement of Affairs and the Appendices, and show examples.

First, the Assignment is a one-page document showing the consumer debtor's name, address, and occupation. It is a legal contract between the consumer debtor and the trustee in bankruptcy. The only substantive paragraph of the document provides that the consumer debtor assigns and abandons all his or her property to the named trustee pursuant to the *Bankruptcy and Insolvency Act*. The consumer debtor signs in front of a witness and then the witness swears or affirms either on the back side of the Assignment or on a separate page that he or she saw the consumer debtor complete the Assignment. See Sample 1.

Second, insofar as the Statement of Affairs is concerned, the front page sets out several different categories of assets that a consumer debtor may own. The consumer debtor is required to set out a brief description of the assets and to estimate the value. Some assets may be exempt; that means, the consumer debtor is entitled to keep the assets and not turn them over to the trustee in bankruptcy. If the consumer debtor is claiming an exempt asset, the designation should be indicated on the form. As indicated in Chapter 6, a consumer

Sample I
ASSIGNMENT FOR GENERAL BENEFIT OF CREDITORS

ASSIGNMENT FOR GENERAL BENEFIT OF CREDITORS

THIS INDENTURE

made in duplicate this _8th_ day of _November, 2014_.

PURSUANT TO THE _BANKRUPTCY AND INSOLVENCY ACT_
BETWEEN

> _Eli Eckler_
> of the City of _Toronto_,
> in the Province of _Ontario_,
> _Bakery Sales Representative_
> hereinafter called "the debtor" of the First Part

> and

> _Samuel Leonard Limited_
> of the City of _Toronto_,
> in the Province of _Ontario_
> hereinafter called "the trustee" of the Second Part.

WHEREAS the consumer debtor is insolvent and desires to assign and to abandon all property for distribution among _his_ creditors in pursuance of the said Act.

NOW THEREFORE THIS INDENTURE WITNESSETH that the consumer debtor does hereby assign, convey and assure unto _Samuel Leonard Limited_ trustee, and to _its_ successors and assigns forever, all _his_ property that is divisible among _his_ creditors under and by virtue of the said Act.

TO HAVE AND TO HOLD all the said property to and for the uses, intents and purposes provided by the said Act.

SIGNED AND SEALED at the City of
Toronto in the Province of _Ontario_
In the presence of

I.M. Witness _____
(Signature of Witness)

Eli Eckler _____
(Signature of Debtor)

SELF-COUNSEL PRESS/14

debtor's assets which are exempt under the laws of the province or territory where the consumer debtor lives do not become the property of the trustee such that the consumer debtor is entitled to keep them. Briefly, such assets generally include clothing, furniture up to a maximum dollar amount, tools and equipment of the person if they are required for his or her living, pension benefits, RRSPs excepting monies paid in to an account within one year of bankruptcy, and in some cases, a homestead exemption.

The list of assets to be declared includes:

- Cash on hand, at home or in the bank
- Furniture
- Personal effects
- Cash surrender value on insurance policies
- Stocks, bonds, and investments
- Real property including house, cottage, and land
- Condominium interests
- Vehicles including automobile, motorcycle, snowmobile, and other types of recreational equipment
- Estimated tax refund
- Other

Unlike the Assignment, the Statement of Affairs is sworn before a commissioner, notary public, or lawyer who will take the consumer debtor's oath or affirmation that the information contained in the Statement of Affairs is true and complete. It is important that the consumer debtor review the Statement carefully since there can be serious consequences if there are any false statements or omissions. If the consumer debtor files false materials, he or she may be liable on summary conviction and face a fine not exceeding $5,000, imprisonment not exceeding one year, or both.

The Statement of Affairs contains a sheet listing the names and addresses of creditors and amounts owed. The consumer debtor should make sure that all creditors are listed, even family and friends. Again, there can be serious consequences if the list is inaccurate. See Sample 2.

Sample 2
STATEMENT OF AFFAIRS

Statement of Affairs
(Paragraph 158(d) of the Act)

IN THE MATTER OF THE BANKRUPTCY OF

Eli Eckler
of the City of *Toronto*,
in the Province of *Ontario*,
Bakery Sales Representative

ASSETS

Type of assets		Description (be specific)	Exempt Property		Estimated Dollar Value
			Yes	No	
1. Cash on hand					
2. Furniture					
3. Personal effects					
4. Cash-surrender value of life insurance policies, RRSPs, etc.					
5. Securities					
6. Real property	House				
	Cottage				
	Land				
7. Motor vehicle	Automobile				
	Motorcycle				
	Snowmobile				
	Other				
8. Recreational equipment					
9. Estimated tax refund					
10. Other assets					
TOTAL					

Date _____

_____ Bankrupt

SELF-COUNSEL PRESS/14

Sample 2 — Continued

LIABILITIES

Creditor	Address	Postal Code	Account No.	Amount of debt		
				Unsecured	Secured	Preferred
1.						
2.						
3.						
4.						
5.						
6.						
7.						
8.						
9.						
10.						
11.						
12.						
13.						
14.						
15.						
16.						
17.						
18.						
19.						
20.						
21.						
22.						
Details of pledged assets		TOTAL	Unsecured			
		TOTAL	Secured			
		TOTAL	Preferred			
TOTAL						

Date _____

_____ Bankrupt

SELF-COUNSEL PRESS/14

Sample 2 — Continued

INFORMATION RELATING TO THE AFFAIRS OF A BANKRUPT

A. PERSONAL DATA

1. Family name	Given names	Date of Birth
		DD/MM/YY

2. Also known as:

3. Complete address including postal code:

4. Marital Status	[ ] Single	[ ] Married	[ ] Separated	[ ] Widowed

5. Full name of spouse:

6. Name of present employer	Occupation (Bankrupt)

7. Dependents (as defined by the *Income Tax Act*)

Number aged 15 or less	Number from 16 to 21	Number of adults (including spouse)

Number of dependents residing with the bankrupt (excluding bankrupt):

8. Have you operated a business within the last 5 years?	Yes	No	(If yes) Type of business

B. WITHIN THE 12 MONTHS PRIOR TO THE DATE OF THE INITIAL BANKRUPTCY EVENT, HAVE YOU...

9A. Sold or disposed of any of your assets?	Yes	No
9B. Made payments in excess of the regular payments to a creditor?	Yes	No
9C. Had any assets seized by a creditor?	Yes	No

C. WITHIN FIVE YEARS PRIOR TO THE DATE OF THE INITIAL BANKRUPTCY EVENT, HAVE YOU...

10A. Sold or disposed of any real estate?	Yes	No
10B. Made any gifts to relatives or others in excess of $500?	Yes	No
10C. Have you made any arrangements to continue to pay any creditors?	Yes	No

Date _____   _____ Bankrupt

SELF-COUNSEL PRESS/14

Sample 2 — Continued

D. BUDGET INFORMATION

11. INCOME		12. EXPENSES	
a. Total earnings		a. Fixed expenses	
b. Financial contributions of all others in the household		b. Others	
c. Other earnings (specify)		c. Payment being made to trustee	
E. TOTAL INCOME		**F. TOTAL EXPENSES**	

13. Have you been bankrupt?

14. If you answered Yes to question 13, when did you received your absolute discharged?

15. Have you ever filed a proposal?

16. If you answered Yes to question 15, when did you file the proposal?

17. Give reasons for your financial difficulty.

18. If your answer is yes to any of questions 8, 9, 10, 13, and 15, give details.

I, _____, of the _____ of _____ in the province of _____, do swear (or solemnly declare) that this statement is to the best of my knowledge a full, true, and complete statement of my affairs on the _____ day of _____ and fully disclose all property of every description that is in my possession or that may devolve on me in accordance with section 67 of the Act.

Sworn (or SOLEMNLY DECLARED)
Before me at the _____ of _____
in the Province of _____ this _____ of
_____, _____.

_____
Commissioner of Oaths
for the Province of
_____

_____
Bankrupt

SELF-COUNSEL PRESS/14

The Statement of Affairs has a sheet containing important information about the consumer debtor's affairs. The information relates to —

- the consumer debtor's full name including given names and birth date;
- the consumer debtor's address;
- the consumer debtor's marital status, whether married, single, widowed, separated, divorced, or common law;
- the consumer debtor's employer's name, and the name of his or her spouse;
- the number of the consumer debtor's dependants and ages;
- whether the consumer debtor has been self-employed within the last five years;
- the consumer debtor's present occupation;
- whether the consumer debtor has transferred any property, made payments in excess of regular payments to a creditor, or had any assets seized by a creditor within the last 12 months;
- whether the consumer debtor has sold any real estate, made any gift to relatives or others in excess of $500 within the last five years;
- whether the consumer debtor has made arrangements to continue to pay any creditors;
- the consumer debtor's net monthly take home pay; and
- costs of fixed expenses.

Sections 9 and 10 of the form are most important. Under the *Bankruptcy and Insolvency Act*, the trustee in bankruptcy is entitled to review all the consumer debtor's transactions within one year of bankruptcy, and in certain cases, within five years. If the consumer debtor is dealing with strangers, then the reviewable period is only three months within the date of bankruptcy. If the consumer debtor is dealing with family members or close friends, then the reviewable period is one year from the date of bankruptcy. If the trustee finds a transaction that is questionable, the trustee may sue the person to recover payment or the property.

A consumer debtor is generally prohibited from giving away or transferring property to another, especially to family members, for little or no value. The trustee is given certain rights and remedies under the Act to recover the property. If the trustee refuses to proceed, creditors can take the action to recover the property.

Again, this may seem repetitive, but it is important. Here are some examples.

- The consumer debtor cannot give his car, having a value of $10,000, to his son five months before going into bankruptcy without receiving $10,000. Technically, this is called a transfer at undervalue.

- If the father owes his son $3,000, he cannot pay him just before bankruptcy if at the time, the father is having financial difficulties paying all the other creditors. This is called a fraudulent preference.

- If the father owes his son $3,000, the father cannot give him the car in payment of the debt. That is also called a transfer at undervalue since the debtor gave a related member, his son, an asset worth $10,000 when only $3,000 was owing to him.

In all of the above examples, whether a transfer at undervalue or a preference, the trustee has the right to sue the son and recover the payment or the car. If the consumer debtor transfers property outside the one-year period, but within five years of bankruptcy, the trustee must prove that the consumer debtor needed the property to pay his or her debts before the transaction will be set aside. There is also provincial legislation that assists the trustee if the transaction took place outside the one-year period.

Chapter 13
HOW DOES THE BANKRUPT LIVE AS AN UNDISCHARGED BANKRUPT?

In this chapter, there is an overview of the effect of bankruptcy on individuals. In comparison, there are no effects on a corporate bankrupt as a corporate bankrupt rarely obtains a discharge or goes back in business under its original name. In many respects, the consumer bankrupt is a disenfranchised person, and he or she is unable to do many things other persons can do.

While the stigma of bankruptcy was considered to be severe many years ago, there is now virtually no stigma for going into bankruptcy. The penalties or the restrictions on being a bankrupt in the 21st century have virtually disappeared. It is not a difficult procedure to go into bankruptcy; the consequences of being bankrupt are not severe and it is relatively easy to get out for most first-time consumers. Most debts incurred by consumer debtors are released or wiped out on discharge.

Living as an undischarged bankrupt, however, comes with certain issues discussed in the following sections.

1. Holding down a Job

There are few restrictions on an individual who is bankrupt from holding positions in corporations or other organizations. An undischarged bankrupt cannot be a Senator of Canada, and cannot be a municipal councillor of a city, town, or municipality. Under provincial law, an undischarged bankrupt may not be a director of a corporation or of a limited liability company.

Probably more restrictive, an undischarged bankrupt cannot hold a licence with many licensing bodies regulated under provincial or federal authorities. For example, an undischarged bankrupt cannot hold a licence from the Canadian Institute of Chartered Accountants, a licence with respect to selling marketable securities, or a licence with respect to selling used vehicles. In these cases, the consumer debtor should consult the governing body that grants the licence. It is imperative that the consumer debtor see a lawyer first before considering filing an assignment in bankruptcy if the consumer debtor holds a licence that may be in jeopardy if there is a bankruptcy. Once the assignment takes place, the undischarged bankrupt will be prohibited from effectively earning a living where he or she has a licence under a governing body that prohibits bankrupts from holding licences.

However, the undischarged bankrupt who holds a licence may not be suspended or lose his or her licence while in bankruptcy. However, if the bankrupt loses his or her licence, the bankrupt may apply for an early discharge hearing on the basis that the bankrupt has lost his or her job and that in order to rehabilitate, he or she needs to get back to work.

2. Telling People about the Bankruptcy

It is necessary that an undischarged bankrupt advise the creditors if he or she engages in any business, obtains credit of more than $1,000, or borrows money. If the undischarged bankrupt does not disclose these facts to the persons with whom he or she enters into any business transaction, then the undischarged bankrupt is potentially guilty of an offence and is punishable on summary conviction to a fine not exceeding $5,000, or to imprisonment for a term not exceeding one year, or to both. Therefore, an undischarged bankrupt should advise third parties that he or she is an undischarged bankrupt before requesting credit.

Similarly, if the consumer bankrupt enters into any transaction with another person for the purposes of obtaining a benefit to which he or she may not be otherwise entitled, then the consumer bankrupt may again be guilty of an offence, and similarly punishable on conviction to a fine not exceeding $5,000, or to imprisonment not exceeding one year, or to both.

Last, if the consumer bankrupt obtains credit over the sum of $1,000 without disclosing to the credit grantor that he or she is an undischarged bankrupt, then such a person may be guilty of an offence and punishable on conviction to a fine not exceeding $5,000, or to imprisonment not exceeding one year, or to both.

3. Living between Bankruptcy and Discharge

While the consumer bankrupt remains undischarged, there are many duties (referred to in more detail in Chapter 8) with which the consumer bankrupt must continue to comply. He or she must disclose and deliver property to the trustee in the case the consumer debtor forgot something or originally misunderstood the duty; complete the Statement of Affairs under oath; attend meetings with the trustee to assist in administering the estate; continue paying surplus income; and generally co-operate with the trustee throughout the administration.

In addition, there are a number of duties and obligations imposed on the consumer bankrupt which if breached may lead to prosecution by the trustee, Superintendent of Bankruptcy, or major creditors.

The following are examples of actions that could lead to prosecution. If the bankrupt —

- without reasonable cause fails to comply with his or her duties as set out in section 158 of the *Bankrupcy and Insolvency Act* and referred to in Chapter 8;

- makes a fraudulent disposition of his or her property either before or after bankruptcy;

- refuses or neglects to answer all questions truthfully;

- makes false entries in the books;

- conceals, destroys, falsifies any books or documents relating to his or her property;

- obtains credit from third parties by false representations; or
- fraudulently conceals or removes property of more than $50 from the bankruptcy estate.

Once the consumer debtor is in bankruptcy, the bankrupt no longer has any control over his or her property. As such, the property of the consumer bankrupt from the date of bankruptcy to the date of discharge technically belongs to the trustee for all creditors. It is called after-acquired property. Such property normally includes a bankrupt's salary or commissions, any winnings from a lottery, and perhaps an inheritance from a family member.

While the consumer bankrupt is undischarged, the trustee is obliged to pursue and attach or seize such after-acquired property for all the creditors.

With respect to salary, if the consumer bankrupt earns $60,000 a year as a salesperson in a retail store, it is likely that the trustee will require that the bankrupt contribute a certain portion of the $60,000 to the trustee for all creditors. The Superintendent of Bankruptcy publishes guidelines, or standards, annually as to how much an individual can afford to pay a trustee. These are only guidelines, and the consumer's way of life together with family responsibilities and dependants must be taken into consideration. The Superintendent's Standards for 2013 are in Appendix III.

If there is a dispute between the consumer bankrupt and the trustee as to the amount of surplus income that should be paid, the trustee or bankrupt may request mediation. The mediator is usually an employee with the Official Receiver's office whose job is to encourage the trustee and the consumer bankrupt to reach a settlement. If the parties cannot reach a settlement as to surplus income, the trustee must apply to the court for an order directing that the consumer bankrupt and the consumer bankrupt's employer pay a certain portion to the trustee for the creditors.

Chapter 14
DISCHARGE: HOW DOES THE BANKRUPT GET OUT OF BANKRUPTCY?

Where the consumer debtor is bankrupt for the first time, then he or she will in most cases be discharged automatically nine months after the date that protection was taken if he or she has no surplus income requirement. If the bankrupt is required to pay surplus income, there is no automatic discharge with the result that there will be a court hearing.

In a small number of cases, it is possible for a consumer debtor to be discharged at any time after three months from the date of the bankruptcy depending on the court list. This earlier discharge may occur where the consumer bankrupt requires a licence from a regulatory body or government to earn a living.

This chapter explains what happens when the consumer debtor, now bankrupt, is ready to get out of bankruptcy or get discharged.

1. Automatic Discharge for First-Time Bankrupts

Parliament amended the *Bankruptcy and Insolvency Act* in 1992 to streamline the bankruptcy process and administration for first-time bankrupts. Where the consumer debtor has realizable assets of less than $15,000, the trustee does not have to mail the notices of the first meeting of creditors by registered mail, and the trustee is not required to place an advertisement of the debtor's bankruptcy in the newspaper in the locality where the debtor resides. Under the Act, an individual bankrupt who has never been bankrupt before may automatically be discharged nine months after the bankruptcy if he or she attends the first two counselling sessions, does not have to pay surplus income, and the trustee reports that his or her conduct is satisfactory.

However, where the trustee, Superintendent, or any creditor who has a proven claim wishes to oppose the discharge of the consumer bankrupt, then the consumer bankrupt must appear in court. In these cases, the automatic provision does not apply. If the bankrupt is required to pay surplus income payments to the estate, and there is no opposition, the automatic discharge is delayed 21 months.

If the bankrupt has not paid the trustee's fees, the trustee may oppose the discharge. This will delay the hearing. The trustee will then proceed to make the application for discharge. This is covered in section **3**.

If the consumer bankrupt requests a third counselling session and the Superintendent agrees, the consumer bankrupt may be provided such services. Counselling sessions are intended to educate and encourage consumers to "control" their spending habits.

2. Automatic Discharge for Second-Time Bankrupts

Second-time bankrupts are entitled to an automatic discharge after 24 months, but if the bankrupt is required to pay surplus income, the discharge is delayed to 36 months.

Bankrupts having debts of more than $200,000 owing to Canada Revenue Agency, representing 75 percent of the total debt, are disqualified from automatic discharge. The bankrupt must file monthly statements of income and expenses with the trustee and must keep current tax returns.

3. Making the Application

If the consumer debtor is not a first-time or second-time bankrupt, the Act provides that there is automatic application for discharge. As a result, there are no special forms required.

In most cases, the trustee in bankruptcy obtains an appointment from the Bankruptcy Court Office for the date on which the discharge will be heard. This date cannot be earlier than 3 months from the date of bankruptcy and no later than 12 months after the bankruptcy. The returnable date, that is, the date when the hearing takes place, will depend on the court sittings and the availability of court time.

Most trustees process the paperwork, and depending on the volume in any particular province or city within the province, the consumer bankrupt can expect to be discharged anywhere between nine months to one year after the application is made if there are no special problems and there is available court time.

The trustee requires that the consumer bankrupt prepare and complete an affidavit of monthly income and expenses. The affidavit sets out the consumer bankrupt's income and his or her normal living expenses. The consumer bankrupt should have the documents to back up the numbers on the affidavit of income and expenses.

Because property or assets purchased by the consumer bankrupt after the date of bankruptcy technically belong to the trustee for the benefit of all creditors, the trustee and the court will want to know whether or not there is any surplus income or other assets that might be available to the creditors. The court looks at the consumer bankrupt's ability to pay in determining whether to make an order on discharge. In addition, the affidavit gives guidance to the court to determine whether or not the consumer bankrupt should be required to make payments to the trustee over a period of time for distribution amongst the creditors as a condition of discharge.

In most cases, the affidavit that the trustee handles and has the bankrupt sign looks something like Sample 3.

In addition to the consumer bankrupt's affidavit of income and expenses, the court will also have the trustee's report on the consumer bankrupt's discharge known as the Section 170 report. The trustee must prepare and file a report to the court with respect to the consumer bankrupt's affairs; the causes of bankruptcy; the manner in which the consumer bankrupt has performed his or her duties; the conduct of the consumer bankrupt both before and after the bankruptcy; whether the consumer bankrupt has been convicted of any offence under the *Bankruptcy and Insolvency Act* and any other act; and matter or circumstance which would justify the court in refusing

Sample 3
AFFIDAVIT OF INCOME AND EXPENSES

Estate no. <u>32-123456</u>

ONTARIO
SUPERIOR COURT OF JUSTICE

IN BANKRUPTCY AND INSOLVENCY

IN THE MATTER OF THE BANKRUPTCY OF

ELI ECKLER
of the City of *Toronto*,
in the Province of *Ontario*,
Bakery Sales Representative

(Summary Administration)

AFFIDAVIT OF INCOME AND EXPENSES

I, <u>*ELI ECKLER*</u>, of the <u>*City*</u> of <u>*Toronto*</u> in the <u>*Province*</u> of <u>*Ontario*</u>, <u>*Bakery Sales*</u>
<u>*Representative*</u>, MAKE OATH AND SAY AS FOLLOWS:

1. I am a bakery sales representative with Sweet Breads Company Limited since
    June 1999 which carries on business in the City of Toronto as a baker of breads,
    bagels, and pastries.

2. I support myself and my two children, ages 10 and 15.

3. I am a salaried employee and earn the sum of $3,345.00 net per month.

4. The following are my approximate monthly expenses:

ITEM	AMOUNT
Rent	$ 1,600.00
Groceries	500.00
Clothing	120.00
Hydro	25.00
Telephone	40.00
Gasoline	100.00
Dentist	50.00
Medications	30.00
Entertainment	100.00
Laundry	35.00
Cleaning	50.00
Child support	600.00
Miscellaneous	50.00
TOTAL	**$ 3,300.00**

Sample 3 — Continued

5. Although some of my monthly expenses vary, I do not have any other monies which would be available to the Trustee for the benefit of creditors. If there is a deficiency in any given month, my former wife contributes that amount.

SWORN before me at the _City_ of)
Toronto, in the _Province_ of _Ontario_,)
this _13th_ day of _September, 2014_ .)
)   _Eli Eckler_
)   Eli Eckler
I.M. Commissioner   )
A Commissioner, etc.

the discharge. The trustee's report is a prescribed form and is filed with the court before the consumer bankrupt's application for discharge. See Sample 4.

The trustee is required to send notice of the application for discharge and the report to the court to all creditors. A creditor can oppose a consumer bankrupt's application by serving a Notice of Opposition at any time prior to the date of the automatic discharge, on the bankrupt, the trustee, and the Superintendent of Bankruptcy. In Ontario, the creditor must pay the Minister of Finance $50 at this time. Once the Bankruptcy Court Office assigns a date for the hearing, the trustee mails notices to all stakeholders.

Once again, the court considers the trustee's report in granting the discharge. In some cases where the trustee opposes the discharge, the trustee sets out the grounds and identifies the conduct on which the trustee's opposition to discharge is based. The trustee's report should include a recommendation as to whether the consumer bankrupt should be discharged subject to conditions having regard to the consumer bankrupt's conduct and ability to pay. In making a recommendation, the trustee considers —

♦ whether the consumer bankrupt paid a portion of his or her surplus income to the estate; or whether the consumer bankrupt was able to pay, but refused to pay;

Sample 4
SECTION 170 REPORT

Estate no. 32-123456

ONTARIO
SUPERIOR COURT OF JUSTICE

IN BANKRUPTCY AND INSOLVENCY

IN THE MATTER OF THE BANKRUPTCY OF

ELI ECKLER
of the City of *Toronto*,
in the Province of *Ontario*

(Summary Administration)

Section 170 Report

Date of Bankruptcy: *7 July 2014*		Date of Initial Bankruptcy Event: *7 July 2013*	
Matrimonial Status: *Married*			
Dependents: *3*	Type of Employment: *bakery sales representative*		
AMOUNT OF LIABILITIES			
	Secured	Preferred	Unsecured
Declared	$0.00	$7,000.00	$66,440.53
Proven	$0.00	$7,000.00	$56,768.09
AMOUNT OF ASSETS			
Description	Value as per Statement of Affairs	Amount Realized	Estimate of Assets to be Realized
	$	$	$ NIL
TOTAL			
ANTICIPATED RATE OF DIVIDENDS			
Preferred creditors:		Unsecured creditors:	

1. Loss of employment: _____
    _____
    _____
    _____

2. Total net monthly income at date of bankruptcy: $ _3,345.00_____

3. Total net monthly income at date of this report: $ _3,345.00_____

4.   Amount established to be paid monthly by the bankrupt: $ _____

5.   Any material changes during period of bankruptcy?

[ ] Yes   [   ] No

(*If yes, provide details*)

6.   Does amount established to be paid correspond with Superintendent's Directive?

[ ] Yes   [   ] No

(*If no, give details of any extenuating circumstances that would affect amount to be paid as per Directive*)

7.   Did bankrupt make all required payments established pursuant to section 68 of the Act?

[ ] Yes   [   ] No

(*If no, provide details*)

8.   Was mediation necessary under subsection 68(6) of 68(7) of the Act to determine amount to be paid by the bankrupt?

[ ] Yes   [   ] No

9.   In the opinion of the trustee, could the bankrupt have made a viable proposal rather than proceeding with bankruptcy?

[ ] Yes   [   ] No

(*If yes, provide details*)

10.   Were duties imposed on bankrupt under the Act performed satisfactorily?

[ ] Yes   [   ] No

11.   Did the bankrupt refuse or neglect to receive counselling?

[ ] Yes   [   ] No

(*If yes, provide details*)

12.   Has the bankrupt previously been bankrupt?

[ ] Yes   [   ] No

(*If yes, provide details*)

13.   Has the bankrupt previously filed a proposal under the *Bankruptcy and Insolvency Act*?

[ ] Yes   [   ] No

(*If yes, provide details*)

14.   Was the conduct of the bankrupt, before or after the date of the initial bankruptcy event, subject to censure?

[ ] Yes   [   ] No

(*If yes, provide details*)

Sample 4 — Continued

15. Did the bankrupt commit any offence in connection with the bankruptcy?

    [ ] Yes   [ ] No

    (*If yes, provide details*)

16. If assets of the bankrupt are not of a value equal to fifty (50) cents on the dollar on the amount of unsecured liabilities, in the trustee's opinion, is it due to circumstances for which the bankrupt cannot justly be held responsible?

    [ ] Yes   [ ] No

    (*If no, provide details*)

17. Other facts, matters, or circumstances that would justify the court in refusing an unconditional Order of Discharge?

    [ ] Yes   [ ] No

    (*If yes, provide details*)

18. Other pertinent information (*e.g., exceptional personal circumstances*)?

    [ ] Yes   [ ] No

19. Is it the intention of the trustee to oppose the bankrupt's discharge for a reason other than those set out in section 170.1 of the Act?

    [ ] Yes   [ ] No

    (*If yes, provide details*)

20. Recommendation of the trustee pursuant to section 170.1 of the Act: (*One box must be checked*)

    [ ]   bankrupt to be discharged without conditions.

    [ ]   bankrupt to be discharged subject to conditions (deemed opposition).

    (*If the second box is checked, give details*)

21. Has the debtor agreed to the conditions recommended by the trustee?

    [ ] Yes   [ ] No

22. If the answer to 21 is No, was the bankrupt made aware of the possibility to request mediation?

    [ ] Yes   [ ] No

23. Was this report approved by the inspectors?

    [ ] Yes   [ ] No

    (*Check one box. If yes, attach the resolution. If no, explain.*)

DATED at *Toronto*, this *7th* day of *July, 2014*.

_____

Samuel Leonard Limited, Trustee

Sample 4 — Continued

ONTARIO
SUPERIOR COURT OF JUSTICE

IN BANKRUPTCY AND INSOLVENCY

IN THE MATTER OF THE BANKRUPTCY OF

Eli Eckler
of the City of *Toronto*,
in the Province of *Ontario*,
Bakery Sales Representative

(Summary Administration)

**TRUSTEE'S REPORT ON BANKRUPT'S
APPLICATION FOR DISCHARGE**

SAMUEL LEONARD LIMITED
Main Street
Toronto, Canada
M6C 2J2

555-555-5555

Sample 4 — Continued

Additional details as required

Number Description of Additional Information

_____

_____

_____

_____

_____

_____

_____

_____

_____

_____

_____

_____

_____

- the total amount paid to the estate regarding his or her debts and financial resources; and

- whether the consumer bankrupt chose bankruptcy as a means to release debts rather than attempting to make a proposal as a means to resolve the financial difficulties.

If the trustee recommends that the consumer bankrupt be discharged subject to a condition, then the consumer bankrupt's application is deemed to be opposed with the result that there will be a hearing. If the trustee has filed a report several months before the hearing, then in Ontario, the trustee also files an updated supplementary report, generally within a week of the hearing.

If the consumer bankrupt contests or disputes any statement contained in the trustee's report or the trustee's recommendation, he or she should notify the trustee of the statements in dispute and contest the report. In this case, the consumer bankrupt can request mediation with respect to the conditions recommended by the trustee.

The mediation hearing usually proceeds before the Official Receiver who determines whether the consumer bankrupt should pay a portion of surplus income to the estate as a condition, and if so, how much. If the issues are not resolved by mediation, then the trustee shall apply to the court for a hearing to decide on the consumer bankrupt's discharge and to determine the matter.

While the trustee's report is considered to be very important for the court, in a last resort, the court decides if and on what terms the consumer bankrupt will be discharged.

4. Prepare for the Hearing when There Are Oppositions

The Superintendent of Bankruptcy, the trustee, and any creditor has a right to oppose the consumer bankrupt's application for discharge. In some cases, the creditor reviews the trustee's report to the court and if the creditor wants to oppose the bankrupt's application on grounds other than set out in the trustee's report, then the creditor must do so by a separate notice of opposition. The creditor must send a copy of the Notice of Opposition to the bankrupt, to the trustee, and to the Office of the Superintendent of Bankruptcy. In some provinces, there may be a filing fee. In the case where the trustee opposes the discharge, the trustee sets out the grounds in its report to the court.

Why would the trustee or a creditor oppose a consumer bankrupt's discharge application? There are several possible reasons.

First, the consumer bankrupt may be earning a sizeable salary from his or her employer and while creditors are generally prevented from seizing part of the salary, the creditor would like the court to make an order requiring the consumer bankrupt to contribute something as a condition of discharge; and this is likely to happen. The court has access to the Superintendent's standards as to the amount of payments that the consumer bankrupt can afford. The amounts depend on how much the consumer bankrupt earns and the number of dependents who are being supported. The standards are published annually to take into consideration fluctuations in the economy. The court takes these standards into account in deciding if, and how much, the bankrupt should pay his or her creditors as a condition of discharge and over what period of time. These monies are not paid to the opposing creditor, but to the trustee for all the creditors. However, the court may award the opposing creditor its costs out of the monies that the bankrupt subsequently pays the trustee.

Second, if the consumer bankrupt owes monies to the Canada Revenue Agency for income tax arrears or for student loans, the court will not be sympathetic to the consumer bankrupt's cause. As a social matter, the court may require the consumer bankrupt to repay more than a nominal amount. The amount depends on how much tax or student loans are owing and the bankrupt's attempts to make payments during the bankruptcy.

Third, the consumer bankrupt may have breached his or her duties as a bankrupt. If the trustee does not proceed criminally against the consumer bankrupt, the court may impose other terms as a condition to the consumer bankrupt's being discharged. For example, the discharge may be suspended for several months in which case the consumer bankrupt remains undischarged until the order takes effect. Practically, this prevents the consumer bankrupt from reapplying for credit cards and the consumer bankrupt's salary will continue to be attached by the trustee in bankruptcy. Another example is where the bankrupt has abused the credit card system: The court may ban the use of credit cards for a period of time or for the rest of his or her life.

Fourth, where the bankrupt has gambled excessively, the court requires that the bankrupt attend counselling sessions and undertake not to gamble in the future. The bankrupt must show that he or she has signed a self-exclusion list and agrees to seek counselling or treatment and refrain from visiting any casino or gambling hall or venue.

Other grounds on which a discharge may be refused, suspended, or granted conditionally include:

+ Failing to keep proper books of account.

+ Failing to account satisfactorily for loss of assets.

+ Incurring unjustifiable extravagances.

+ Continued gambling.

+ Entering a frivolous or vexatious defence to an action, or forcing the creditor to incur significant legal fees in prosecuting the action.

+ Entering into an unfair creditor preference within three months of bankruptcy.

+ Being bankrupt on a previous occasion.

+ Committing fraud or fraudulent breach of trust.

+ Failing to perform the duties of an undischarged bankrupt.

+ Failing to comply with an obligation to pay a portion of surplus income to the estate.

+ Choosing to file an assignment into bankruptcy rather than attempting to make a proposal to creditors as a means of resolving the debts.

If the discharge is opposed by the trustee, any creditor, or the Superintendent's office, the trustee obtains a date from the court and then notifies the creditor or the Superintendent's office of the date and time of the hearing.

The initial application for discharge is usually made before the registrar or Deputy Registrar in Bankruptcy. The registrar has the authority to hear discharge applications and can make such decisions as are permitted by the bankruptcy judge. Ordinarily, the bankruptcy office determines which judicial officer hears the discharge application. (See Sample 5.)

Sample 5
NOTICE OF OPPOSITION TO DISCHARGE

ONTARIO
SUPERIOR COURT OF JUSTICE

IN BANKRUPTCY AND INSOLVENCY

IN THE MATTER OF THE BANKRUPTCY OF

ELI ECKLER
of the City of *Toronto*,
in the Province of *Ontario*,
Bakery Sales Representative

(Summary Administration)

NOTICE OF OPPOSITION TO DISCHARGE

TAKE NOTICE that pursuant to subsection 170(7) of the *Bankruptcy and Insolvency Act*, R.S.C. 1985, Chapter B-3, as amended, the Regal Bank of Canada opposes the discharge of the bankrupt in this matter on the following grounds among other grounds:

(a)   the assets of the bankrupt are not of a value equal to fifty (50) cents on the dollar on the amount of the bankrupt's unsecured liabilities and the bankrupt has not adequately explained the difference;

(b)   the earnings of the bankrupt may reasonably be expected to become and be sufficient to meet a part or all indebtedness incurred;

(c)   the bankrupt failed to account for his assets;

(d)   the bankrupt has gambled;

(e)   the bankrupt has paid one creditor who is a relative when other creditors were not paid;

(f)   such further and other grounds as Counsel may advise or the Court permit.

DATED at <u>Toronto</u>, this <u>19th</u> day of <u>June</u>, <u>2014</u>.

ROBERT & STANLEY
Barristers and Solicitors
Suite 600
50 Main Street West
Toronto, Ontario
M5K 2X9
Tel: 555-555-5555
Solicitors for the Regal Bank of Canada

SELF-COUNSEL PRESS/14

5. Attend at the Bankruptcy Court

In view of the wide discretion that a court has in granting or refusing a discharge, it is recommended that the consumer bankrupt retain a bankruptcy lawyer to attend with him or her at the discharge hearing.

As most consumer debtors are unfamiliar with the judicial system, it may be advisable for him or her to attend the bankruptcy court on other discharge hearing dates so as to become familiar with the process, and the types of questions that the court, creditors, and lawyers may put to the debtor at the hearing. Often, this preview will assist the consumer debtor in appearing in court on his or her date of discharge.

Most hearings take about one half hour or less. However, where the opposing creditor has a lawyer, or has prepared a detailed presentation, the hearing will extend to about two hours or longer if there are several witnesses. The trustee will be able to gauge how long the hearing will take, and apart from simple ones, the trustee will request a special appointment initially for two hours. If the opposing creditor is a corporation, the court may require that it obtain legal counsel, although in some cases with the permission of the court, a paralegal or law clerk can represent the corporation.

Prior to the hearing date, the consumer bankrupt should review the trustee's report to the court and any Notice of Opposition. The bankrupt should be prepared to answer questions about all the grounds opposing his or her discharge set out in the trustee's report and in the Notice of Opposition. The bankrupt should bring all his or her documents supporting the income and expense statement and documents that may rebut the grounds set out in the opposition. While each case is fact specific, the bankrupt must review each ground carefully and be prepared to answer.

If the discharge application proceeds, the court may —

♦ grant the discharge,

♦ refuse the discharge,

♦ suspend the operation of the discharge for a period of time,

♦ impose terms of the bankrupt as a condition of discharge, such as the payment of money, or

♦ suspend the discharge and impose terms.

In many cases, where the consumer bankrupt earns more than a reasonable allowance for his or her station in life or anticipates having a higher income, the court may order the consumer bankrupt to pay a certain amount of money to the trustee over a period of time as a condition to discharge. Once the consumer bankrupt has paid the amount, the court will grant an absolute discharge. Alternatively, it is common for the court to grant the discharge at the hearing on the condition that the consumer bankrupt consents to a judgment for the amount that is to be paid over time. If the consumer bankrupt consents to the judgment, then he or she will be discharged immediately. If the consumer bankrupt does not sign the consent to judgment, the consumer bankrupt remains undischarged.

If the consumer bankrupt signs the consent, he or she is entitled to an immediate discharge. The judgment remains unsatisfied until it is paid. If the consumer defaults in payments, the trustee can proceed to enforce the judgment in the usual ways available to creditors. If after one year the bankrupt is having difficulty in making payments to the trustee, the bankrupt may apply to the court for an order modifying the earlier order. However, if the debtor makes no attempt to satisfy the judgment, the trustee can bring an application to set aside the discharge, putting the debtor back into bankruptcy.

If the bankruptcy arises out of a failure to pay a judgment on a motor vehicle accident, the provincial authorities, in Ontario at least, will not allow the discharged bankrupt to renew his or her driver's licence until there is a payment or some form of settlement.

If the consumer bankrupt has breached his or her duties under the Act (see Chapter 8, and section 158 of the Act in Appendix I), the court may refuse the discharge completely, especially where the bankrupt has breached several duties and has generally not co-operated with the trustee.

At the hearing for discharge, it is customary for the consumer bankrupt to take the stand and give his or her testimony regarding the affairs of the bankruptcy, the causes of bankruptcy, and other such information so as to give the court an opportunity to evaluate and decide which one of the above types of orders to make. The consumer bankrupt will be sworn on the new or old testament, or Koran, to tell the whole truth, or in some cases of different religious beliefs, the bankrupt may affirm that the evidence that he or she is about to give is the whole truth. The registrar or judge may request further information about the consumer bankrupt's assets and liabilities and prospects for earning. If the bankrupt requires an interpreter, the bankrupt should notify the trustee and arrange for a certified interpreter to appear at the hearing.

The opposing creditor may cross-examine the consumer bankrupt as to his or her conduct prior to and during the bankruptcy. The consumer bankrupt should have bills, invoices, and other documents to show the court and others of the various expenses referred to in the affidavit. The court will not, for example, require that the consumer bankrupt make a payment to the trustee for creditors where the consumer bankrupt has a large family and a modest income. Except in unusual circumstances, a contested hearing lasts less than two hours.

In exercising its discretion to grant or refuse a discharge, the court considers the interests of the creditors, the interests of the debtor, and the protection of the public in the bankruptcy system. While the honest, but unfortunate debtor requires rehabilitation and reform, and the need to start afresh, the creditors also need to know that their rights are not being abused. In balancing these rights, the court must consider the integrity of the bankruptcy system.

The order of discharge releases a consumer bankrupt from most claims provable in bankruptcy. However, a discharged bankrupt is not released from those items set out in Chapter 7. These will include claims based on fines, restitution orders, claims based on fraudulent conduct and misrepresentation, and support orders made in favour of spouses and children.

For creditors who want to oppose the consumer bankrupt's discharge on the basis that their claim is based on a claim that will survive discharge, the usual procedure is to wait until the consumer bankrupt is discharged and then proceed in the ordinary courts. The court will not deal with this type of matter on an application for discharge.

Once the consumer bankrupt has been discharged, he or she can assume all functions of an undischarged person. For example, the discharged bankrupt can become a director of a corporation or can apply for a licence under a governing body, whereas before bankruptcy, an individual could not hold a licence.

Within six months, the consumer should be able to apply for new credit cards. Some companies or banks may require a second applicant for a while until the consumer reestablishes a credit line. The consumer should send a copy of the discharge order as soon as possible to any credit card reporting agencies to start the process of restoring his or her credit.

If the court orders the bankrupt to pay a sum of money over time, and the bankrupt is unable to make those payments, the bankrupt may apply after one year for an order varying the discharge. This hearing is not an appeal of the decision. At this second hearing one year later, the bankrupt will have to show that there is no reasonable probability of being able to comply with the terms of the discharge. The court will review what the bankrupt has done within the last year in attempting to make payments, the bankrupt's ability to make the payments, and the bankrupt's credibility. If the court considers that the bankrupt will not be able to make the payments, the court can vary the original order of payment.

Chapter 15
COMMON QUESTIONS

Many questions are asked of lawyers, accountants, and trustees before, during, and after bankruptcy. The questions relate to all parts of the bankruptcy process. They are not set out in any particular order. In some cases, the answers to these questions can be found elsewhere in this book, but for the sake of answering the most common questions which arise frequently, the answers are gathered into this one chapter.

1. Who Prepares the Consumer Debtor's Income Tax Returns? What Happens to a Refund?

A bankrupt's tax year is divided into two parts. If a consumer debtor files an assignment, for example, on May 1, then the tax year is divided into the period between January 1 and April 30, and the second part is the period between May 1 and December 31, known as the post-bankruptcy return.

In most cases, the trustee in bankruptcy prepares the income tax returns for the consumer debtor for two periods of time; that is, pre-bankruptcy and post-bankruptcy until the end of the calendar year.

With the pre-bankruptcy return, it is possible in many cases of consumer debtors that there will be a tax refund available. As the consumer debtor has a duty to deliver up all property to the trustee, the tax refund belongs to the estate. That tax refund is technically property of the bankruptcy estate and the trustee receives it on the consumer debtor's behalf and deposits it into the estate bank account. Therefore, the trustee will ask the consumer debtor to sign a direction to Canada Revenue Agency permitting the Agency to pay the trustee although technically the trustee is entitled to the refund. However, if there is money owing to Canada Revenue Agency at the date of bankruptcy, the Agency will set the refund off against the debt.

With the post-bankruptcy return, the trustee may, but need not, prepare the consumer debtor's bankruptcy return for at least one year after bankruptcy. Once again, if there is a refund, the trustee is entitled to intercept that refund and pay it into the estate for the general distribution to creditors. Canada Revenue Agency is not entitled to set the refund off against any tax debt owed prior to bankruptcy. As for subsequent years, the bankrupt may request that the trustee prepare the tax returns or alternatively the bankrupt may employ someone else to complete them.

2. Is Notice of the Consumer Debtor's Bankruptcy Published in the Newspaper?

In most consumer bankruptcies, where the net realizable assets are less than $15,000, the trustee proceeds under what is called the Summary Administration provisions of the *Bankruptcy and Insolvency Act*. Those provisions allow the trustee to cut costs in the administration. For example, instead of sending notices to creditors by registered mail, the trustee can send notices by ordinary post, fax, or email. Likewise for publication in newspapers; in Summary Administrations, there is generally no obligation on the trustee to publish notice of the bankruptcy in a newspaper.

However, if the assets exceed $15,000, then the estate is administered under the ordinary provisions of the *Bankruptcy and Insolvency Act*. In that case, there must be a notice published in a local newspaper in the area in which the consumer debtor resides. The notice in the newspaper advises the public that there has been a bankruptcy, whether by assignment or by bankruptcy order, and that the first meeting of creditors is set for a certain date. It also advises creditors that they may file their proofs of claim on or before the meeting.

Within five days of bankruptcy, the trustee must prepare a notice to creditors if there is going to be a meeting of creditors. If the trustee cannot compile the list within that time, the trustee must obtain an order extending the time to call a meeting of creditors.

3. Can Creditors Continue to Call on the Consumer Debtor for Payment after Bankruptcy?

Once the consumer debtor is placed into bankruptcy, any creditor with a provable claim is prohibited from proceeding with any action against the consumer debtor. In other words, the creditor cannot start or continue any lawsuit to collect on the debt. That creditor needs permission of the court, technically called "leave of the court" to do so and in almost all cases, the court will not give the creditor that permission.

Once creditors know that the consumer debtor is bankrupt, they will stop harassing the consumer debtor and not send demand letters for payment. All institutional creditors know the bankruptcy process and they will not bother the consumer debtor anymore. These creditors will work through the trustee in bankruptcy if they foresee a problem or obtain a special order of the court if the trustee refuses or they have a special claim that may survive the consumer debtor's discharge.

In some cases, creditors will have claims that will survive bankruptcy discharge. Those claims, as set out in Chapter 7, relate to fines and penalties; claims for alimony, maintenance, and support; claims based on fraud or misrepresentation; or claims for breach of trust while acting as a fiduciary. In these types of claims, the creditor can sue the bankrupt after the bankrupt has been discharged. If the creditor wishes to proceed earlier than that, then the creditor requires a special order or leave of the court to do so.

4. Will the Consumer Debtor's Employer Find Out about the Bankruptcy?

An employee can continue to work even though he or she has gone bankrupt. However, where the employee earns a wage which is more than capable of supporting his or her family, then the trustee must request that the bankrupt contribute a portion of his or her salary for the benefit of all the creditors. There is a provision under the

Bankruptcy and Insolvency Act which allows the trustee to demand and receive such payment from the bankrupt and the bankrupt's employer. The trustee is guided by the Superintendent's standards, that is a sliding scale of amounts based on income and the number of dependents. If the employee disputes the amount of surplus income that should be paid to the estate, then the trustee must submit the dispute to mediation. The mediator is usually an employee in the Official Receiver's office or someone approved by the Superintendent's office. The mediator attempts to resolve the dispute and fix an amount that will be agreeable to both the bankrupt and the trustee. If that is not possible, the trustee may apply to the Bankruptcy Court for an order determining the amount of surplus income that should be paid to the trustee.

Even when the consumer debtor's employer finds out about the bankruptcy, it is illegal for the employer to dismiss the consumer debtor solely on the grounds that the consumer debtor has filed an assignment or that a bankruptcy order has been made, unless his or her employment is dependent on a licence such as an accountant or a real estate broker. The consumer debtor would have to check with provincial and territorial laws to determine whether the licence is terminated or suspended on bankruptcy.

5. Is the Consumer Debtor's Credit Rating Affected?

When a consumer debtor files an assignment in bankruptcy, the trustee requests that the consumer debtor turn over all his or her credit cards. Each holder of the credit card will be notified of the bankruptcy and as a general rule, there will be no further extension of credit. While the consumer debtor is an undischarged bankrupt, the consumer debtor cannot borrow any money over $1,000 without revealing that the consumer debtor is an undischarged bankrupt.

Once the consumer bankrupt is discharged, however, the consumer's credit rating will be returned assuming that the requirements of the holder of the credit card can be met. Usually within one year of a bankrupt's discharge, the consumer will be able to obtain new credit cards. However, if this is a second bankruptcy or there are special problems arising out of the bankruptcy, there may be some difficulty in re-establishing credit. Credit reporting agencies, such as Equifax and TransUnion, may be consulted by credit card companies before issuing new credit cards. Once discharged, the consumer should contact and advise the credit reporting company of the particulars of discharge, namely, the date, court, judge, and any conditions that may have been imposed and satisfied.

6. What Happens to the Consumer Debtor's Bank Accounts?

On bankruptcy, all the consumer debtor's property automatically vests in the trustee. That means that the consumer debtor's property is placed in the hands of the trustee for the administration. Therefore, the consumer debtor has a duty to deliver up his or her property to the trustee. For example, the consumer debtor's bank accounts technically belong to the trustee since the bank owes the consumer debtor the money. The monies in those bank accounts must be turned over as soon as possible after the assignment in bankruptcy is made. The trustee notifies the bank on filing the assignment.

Once the consumer bankrupt receives a paycheque for the period subsequent to the date of bankruptcy, that money may be deposited into the consumer bankrupt's bank account. The trustee in bankruptcy will not attach that amount or request that the consumer bankrupt pay that sum to the estate. However, in a case where the consumer bankrupt earns more than a reasonable amount, the trustee will require that the consumer bankrupt pay the surplus income or turn over a portion of the salary to the trustee for the benefit of creditors. The Superintendent publishes standards each year. The standards are the scale which the trustee uses in determining whether the consumer bankrupt can afford to pay any monies to the creditors while the consumer bankrupt is undischarged (see Appendix III).

7. Where Can the Consumer Debtor Learn Better Budgeting Skills?

Unfortunately, most people do not learn budgeting skills in high school, community college, or university. These skills are learned on the job and in the home. It is necessary for people to budget their net paycheque on a weekly, biweekly, or monthly basis. People should review their usual monthly expenses and make sure that there is enough money for each of the proposed expenses. If there is not enough money to cover all those expenses, then apart from borrowing on their credit cards or from some other source, they should consider cutting back on particular items or even doing without them.

Needless to say, the expenses vary from person to person and from family to family and from community to community. Proper budgeting methods are critical to everyone as there is a natural tendency to spend without having sufficient income to pay the expenses.

In most provinces, there are also credit counselling services where trained counsellors teach the consumer debtor on a regular basis how to budget the bank account and monies received from employment. Where possible, the consumer debtor should consult the Yellow Pages for credit counselling in the area where she or he lives. It is often an agency of United Way.

Prior to going into bankruptcy, or perhaps not at all, the trustee in bankruptcy must give the consumer debtor a counselling session. The trustee or a qualified counsellor discusses with the consumer debtor money management, spending and shopping habits, warning signs of financial difficulties, and the use of credit cards. The session may be alone with the trustee or in a group.

8. Can the Consumer Debtor Get a Loan after the Bankruptcy?

The answer to whether a consumer debtor can obtain a loan after discharge is "yes." Once the consumer debtor is discharged from bankruptcy, the consumer debtor is released from all provable debts in bankruptcy. That is, all the claims of creditors are released or discharged except for those that survive bankruptcy. Only those claims relating to fines and penalties, alimony, maintenance or support, fraud or misrepresentation survive the bankruptcy. Therefore, as the consumer debtor is unlikely to have any other debt, the consumer debtor may be able to obtain a loan from any lending institution based on salary qualifications, or in other words, if the debtor can show that he or she can carry the loan or line of credit from a steady job.

9. Are the Assets of the Consumer Debtor's Spouse Affected?

The bankruptcy affects only the person who goes bankrupt. So spouses and partners who have co-signed a credit card application remain liable for the balance. However, if the consumer debtor conveys or transfers property to his or her spouse for a value that is lower than its fair market value within one year prior to bankruptcy, then it is likely that the trustee, or the creditors in certain circumstances, will proceed to set aside the conveyance or transfer. The trustee can attach those assets that have been conveyed away or transferred to the spouse or to any other person who has not paid fair market value. These are transfers at undervalue and fraudulent preferences under the *Bankruptcy and Insolvency Act*. There is also provincial legislation similar to these remedies.

If there is a discharge hearing, the bankrupt will be required to submit a statement of income and expenses on a monthly basis to the trustee. The statement of income usually includes the net income of the spouse. In fixing an amount to be paid by the bankrupt as a condition of discharge, the court looks at the combined income, the expenses, and the Superintendent's standards. As a result, it is possible that the court will consider the spouse's income in setting an amount that the bankrupt should pay as a condition of discharge.

10. Where Does the Consumer Debtor Find a Bankruptcy Lawyer and/or Trustee?

Bankruptcy lawyers are generally prohibited from advertising their specialty in the Yellow Pages or any other form of public newspaper or magazine. Nonetheless, they may place their name as a lawyer in the Yellow Pages, other telephone directory, on their website, and in good taste in the newspaper. The Canadian Bar Association, both provincially and nationally, has a bankruptcy and insolvency section. Members of the Association can direct the consumer debtor to a member of the section.

If the consumer debtor does not know a bankruptcy practitioner, he or she can be referred to one by a friend, but the consumer debtor is best to see a general practitioner and have him or her refer the consumer debtor to the bankruptcy specialist. The bankruptcy specialist can give the consumer debtor answers to most, if not all, of the consumer debtor's questions.

A bankruptcy lawyer, or a general practitioner, can give the consumer debtor a selection of names of trustees. While a licensed trustee can administer a consumer bankruptcy, sub-specialties have developed within the profession. Most general practitioners, lawyers and accountants, will probably not know the distinction. However, bankruptcy specialists within the area will know that some practise in the area of consumer bankruptcies while others service only corporate debtors, and yet still others give management or receivership advice. Obviously, the consumer debtor should pick the appropriate trustee for his or her own needs.

Trustees may advertise, and they do so in personal columns in newspapers, magazines, on the Internet, and generally in any form of literature that is circulated to the public. The trustee becomes involved in restructuring debts whether the problems are small consumer-oriented ones or problems in mega-insolvencies. Licensed trustees also become involved in formal arrangements, receiverships, and liquidations. They may even be consulted without any type of appointment. Sometimes, it may be easier to go to a trustee and then ask the trustee for a shortlist of lawyers if the consumer debtor or the trustee suspects difficulties.

II. Does the Consumer Debtor Have Any Director's Liabilities?

The consumer debtor may be involved in corporate businesses. The consumer debtor may be a small-business person who qualifies as a "consumer" debtor for the purposes of the Act. As a result, the consumer debtor may be a director or officer of a corporation, and as such, incur liability.

In the case of a corporate bankruptcy, many provincial and federal statutes governing taxes and employee benefits make the directors liable for the corporate debt if the corporation fails to deduct and remit the taxes to the proper authority. In Ontario, for example, there are more than 100 federal and provincial statutes that have sections dealing with liabilities of an insolvent corporation. These statutes cover retail sales tax, vacation pay, employee wages and related benefits, health tax, the employees' portion of income tax, Canada pension, employment insurance premiums, and the goods and services tax. Taxes owing on income tax, Canada pension, and employment insurance are special and virtually, with minor exceptions, have priority over all the consumer debtor's assets including real estate regardless of whether the consumer debtor is in receivership or bankruptcy or both.

While these statutes impose liability on directors, many of them give the directors a defence of "due diligence"; the directors may have taken every reasonable step to pay the tax but in view of the declining business they were unable to do so. There is much case law in this area of director liability. Each statute must be examined carefully to see whether this defence exists and to see how the case law has developed in determining the nature of the defence.

In addition to the due diligence defence, directors may also be protected under the general discretionary power to pursue directors. Governments do not necessarily take legal action against the directors of a bankrupt corporation every time there is a bankruptcy unless the corporation has flagrantly, negligently, or fraudulently disregarded the laws and the enforcement and compliance sections. If the consumer debtor is a director, it is best to —

- direct that tax payments be deducted and remitted when required,
- verify with the bookkeeper or accountant that the taxes have been paid on a regular basis,
- set up a special trust,
- obtain broad insurance,
- obtain an indemnity supported by security against the corporation's assets, and
- be aware of what the other directors are doing.

12. Can the Consumer Debtor Keep the Vehicle after Bankruptcy?

If the consumer debtor owns his or her vehicle, it must be turned over to the trustee in bankruptcy on filing the assignment as property of the estate. However, if the vehicle is required for business, then it can be declared as an exempt item, or technically as a tool of the trade. The exemption varies in each province, and the exemptions are generally very low. For example, in Ontario, the consumer debtor can keep the vehicle if its value does not exceed $5,650.

If the vehicle is leased, bankruptcy generally terminates all contracts between the consumer debtor and third parties. The leasing company will, in most cases under its lease, have the right to repossess the vehicle, sell it, and then claim any deficient balance in the bankrupt estate. However, if the bankrupt is not in arrears, the bankrupt may be able to continue making payments under the lease and keep the lease in good standing. Such payments will depend on the size of the payments, type of vehicle, and cash flow. The trustee on behalf of the creditors may object to these payments if they are sizeable in relation to the bankrupt's income and expenses and the type of vehicle. For example, if the bankrupt leases a 2013 Jaguar at $1,100 a month, the trustee will object and will require the bankrupt return the car to the dealer. However, if the car is 15 years old and the leasing payments are $300 a month, the trustee will not challenge the contract.

13. When Can the Consumer Debtor Get back His or Her Credit Cards?

As indicated earlier, once the consumer bankrupt is discharged, the consumer can apply for credit cards. However, the credit card issuer may require proof that the consumer debtor has been discharged and may require another person to be responsible for the payments. As expected, the credit card issuer will slowly advance credit upon being satisfied that the now discharged bankrupt will be able to make the payments.

14. How Are Student Debts Treated?

A debtor who owes money for student loans borrowed from the federal or any of the provincial or territorial governments can list the agency as a creditor. The enforcement of the student loans is suspended while the debtor is in bankruptcy protection and even after discharge up to seven years from the date the student left school. However, where the student has and will have financial difficulty in paying back the loan and has acted in good faith, the student can apply to the court for an order discharging the debt within the seven-year period.

GLOSSARY

APPLICATION FOR A BANKRUPTCY ORDER: The application for a bankruptcy order is the initiating document that is issued by the court to place a debtor into bankruptcy. Formerly, this application was called a petition for a receiving order.

ASSETS: Assets are property which the debtor owns, anywhere in Canada and outside Canada. Assets comprise personal property and real property. Personal property is usually tangible, that is one can pick it up and carry it, compared to property that is intangible which is something like a promissory note, the paper showing that the debtor owes money to someone. Real property includes the debtor's home, farm, or cottage. In a bankruptcy situation, the debtor does not have sufficient assets to pay all the debts.

ASSIGNMENT: This is the document that the debtor signs when going into bankruptcy. It is called an Assignment in bankruptcy and it is filed with the Official Receiver in the area in which the debtor lives or carries on business. It is a voluntary act; that is, the debtor files the Assignment rather than an involuntary act which is the legal remedy of the creditor.

BAILIFF: The bailiff is the person who acts usually on behalf of a landlord. The bailiff's job is to seize or take the debtor's property if the debtor fails to pay the rent. A bailiff may also act for a city in the collection of overdue property taxes.

BANKRUPTCY: Bankruptcy is the state of being bankrupt under the *Bankruptcy and Insolvency Act*. It means that the debtor is insolvent and is unable to pay all the debts as they fall due or it means that the debtor does not have enough property which if sold would be sufficient to pay the debts. Most business bankruptcies are conducted under the ordinary provisions of the Act. Most consumer bankruptcies are conducted under the Summary Administration provisions of the Act which provide for inexpensive steps being taken to administer the estate.

BANKRUPTCY AND INSOLVENCY ACT: This Act is federal legislation which applies across Canada from Newfoundland to British Columbia and the three territories. It is legislation that governs all bankruptcies and proposals. It has marginal effects over receiverships and does not affect liquidations.

BANKRUPTCY ORDER: A bankruptcy order is the order that is made on a successful application for bankruptcy. A creditor applies to the court for a bankruptcy order and once made, the debtor is officially bankrupt.

BULK SALES: Bulk sales is the sale of substantially all the assets, the bulk, of a company and in order to protect the buyer, the seller must comply with the provisions of the *Bulk Sales Act*.

CHATTEL MORTGAGE: This is a form of security whereby the debtor, chattel mortgagor, grants to the chattel mortgagee, secured creditor, security over certain personal property for the repayment of a debt. Chattel mortgages are technically no longer used in most provinces; however, some companies still use the forms. It has been replaced by the security agreement under the *Personal Property Security Act* (PPSA).

CREDITOR: A creditor is a person or company who lends money, or supplies goods or services to the debtor (the buyer). There are generally three types of creditors. First, the creditor may be secured; that is, the creditor holds some form of property of the debtor as security for the repayment of the debt; second, the creditor may be unsecured with no special rights or privileges; and last, the creditor may be preferred, that is it has special status under legislation over unsecured creditors, but not as high as secured creditors.

DEBTOR: The person (the buyer) who owes money for receiving money, goods, or services.

DEEMED TRUST: A trust which notionally carves an amount of money out of a business debtor's property as though the debtor collected and kept that amount separate and apart from his or her other property is called a deemed trust. It is usually associated with a statutory deemed trust in favour of the Crown for such taxes as Canada Pension, employment insurance premiums, and income tax. There is also a deemed trust for HST/GST.

DISCHARGE: When an individual goes bankrupt, the individual can get out of bankruptcy usually within a year. For first-time bankrupts, there is an automatic discharge after nine months unless there is an objection. The process of getting out of bankruptcy is called a discharge. The order may be an absolute order, a suspended order, or a conditional order with the condition usually being a payment or payments of money.

DISTRESS: In commercial tenancies, distress is the right of a commercial landlord to seize and sell the tenant's property for arrears of rent.

ESTATE: When an individual goes bankrupt, his or her property becomes an estate controlled and administered by the trustee in bankruptcy.

EXAMINATIONS: There are examinations by the Official Receiver and by the trustee under the *Bankruptcy and Insolvency Act* as well as by any creditor who obtains an order from the court. The examination can touch on any matter relating to the bankruptcy estate or the property of the debtor within five years of the date of bankruptcy. In all consumer bankruptcies, the Official Receiver may examine the bankrupt.

EXEMPTIONS: The debtor is entitled to exemptions according to the laws of the province or territory where he or she resides at the date of bankruptcy. The exemptions vary from province to province and territory. A corporation is not entitled to any exemptions.

FRAUDULENT CONVEYANCE: This is a conveyance, transfer, or gift of property to another for little or no consideration made with the intent to defeat, hinder, delay, or defraud creditors or others. It is governed by the *Fraudulent Conveyances Act*. It is usually made between persons who are related or closely connected under suspicious circumstances.

FRAUDULENT PREFERENCE: Under the *Bankruptcy and Insolvency Act*, it is a conveyance or transfer of property or payment by the debtor to a creditor within 3 months of bankruptcy, or if related, within 12 months, at a time when the debtor was insolvent and had the intent to prefer one creditor over others. If these conditions occur, the trustee in bankruptcy has the right to recover the property from the creditor. In addition, a preference may occur under the provincial *Assignment and Preferences Act* or similar legislation.

GARNISHMENT: This is a legal process whereby a judgment creditor can attach or seize monies owing to the judgment debtor. First, however, the creditor must proceed through the court and obtain a judgment. Then, the judgment creditor can notify a debtor's employer to pay a portion of the debtor's wages to the judgment creditor. If the employer refuses to do so, the employer will likely have to pay twice.

GUARANTEE: A guarantee is an agreement under which a third person, the guarantor, agrees to pay the creditor if the debtor fails to do so. Many guarantee forms make the guarantor directly liable with the debtor, or in other words, the guarantee is really not a guarantee at all, but a joint promise to pay the creditor. Compare a guarantee with an indemnity.

INDEMNITY: An indemnity is an agreement under which a third party agrees to pay the creditor directly irrespective of whether the debtor can or does pay the creditor.

INSOLVENT: Insolvent means the state of having more liabilities than assets, or ceasing to meet liabilities as they generally fall due. All bankrupts are insolvent, but all insolvents are not necessarily bankrupt.

INSPECTOR: An inspector is a person who is appointed under the *Bankruptcy and Insolvency Act* to represent the creditors. There can be one to five inspectors in an estate and an inspector need not be a creditor. In consumer bankruptcies, there is rarely an inspector appointed.

JUDGMENT DEBTOR EXAMINATION: It is an examination under oath, and is usually referred to as a "JD," or an examination in aid of execution, taken by the judgment creditor after judgment is obtained.

OFFICIAL RECEIVER: The Official Receiver is a representative of the Superintendent of Bankruptcy under the *Bankruptcy and Insolvency Act*. The Official Receiver accepts the filing of an assignment in bankruptcy and a proposal. He or she chairs the first meeting of creditors in a bankruptcy or can delegate that function to the trustee.

OFFICIAL RECEIVER'S EXAMINATION: In some consumer bankruptcies, the Official Receiver conducts an examination of the business debtor or director if the debtor is a corporation with respect to the bankrupt's conduct, the causes of bankruptcy, and the disposition of the bankrupt's property. There are prescribed questions to the questionnaire. In addition, the Official Receiver may receive questions from the trustee and from creditors.

ORDINARY CREDITOR: An ordinary creditor is a creditor who has supplied credit to the debtor and may be referred to as a trade creditor, an unsecured creditor, or judgment creditor. Compare this term with preferred creditor and secured creditor.

POWER OF SALE: A contractual or statutory right of a secured creditor such as a mortgagee to sell the debtor's property after default on notice to the debtor and to all interested persons.

PREFERRED CREDITOR: A type of creditor governed under section 136 of the *Bankruptcy and Insolvency Act* which gives the creditor priority in payment over ordinary unsecured creditors such as the trustee's fees and expenses and the claims of support creditors or recipients.

PROPOSAL: A proposal is an agreement between the debtor and his or her creditors pursuant to the *Bankruptcy and Insolvency Act* whereby the debtor makes a composition of the debts, requests an extension of time to pay the creditors, or proposes a scheme of arrangement to satisfy the claims of creditors. Under the Act, a business may file a proposal under Division 1 of Part III or a consumer may file a proposal under Division II of Part III.

RECEIVER (AND MANAGER): A receiver and manager is the person or corporation who is appointed to take possession and sell the debtor's assets in a receivership. A secured creditor may appoint a receiver under an instrument or may apply to the court for an appointment of a receiver. Where the receiver is appointed under the *Bankruptcy and Insolvency Act*, the receiver must hold a valid licence as a trustee in bankruptcy. This assures the public that the receiver will be accountable.

RECEIVERSHIP: Receivership is the process whereby all or substantially all of the debtor's assets are seized and may be sold if the debtor fails to pay pursuant to a security instrument or court order. If a receivership is invoked pursuant to a security instrument, it is referred to as a private appointment, or if it is invoked pursuant to a statutory authority, it is referred to as a court appointment. It is not common to have a receivership of an individual.

SECURED CREDITOR: This is a creditor who holds a lien, mortgage, or charge against the debtor's assets or collateral as security for the repayment of the debt.

STATUTORY LIEN: A statutory lien is a lien that is given by statute to enhance priority over ordinary creditors such as tax liens.

STAY OF PROCEEDINGS: This is the phrase that is given to the stage of an action, application, or other legal proceeding which cannot proceed without an order of the court.

SUMMARY ADMINISTRATION: This is the type of administration of a bankrupt estate where the assets do not exceed $15,000, where registered mail is not required, where notice of the bankruptcy is not published, and where there are usually no inspectors.

SUPERINTENDENT OF BANKRUPTCY: The Superintendent is the person who monitors the trustee's administration of bankrupt estates and controls the licensing of trustees. The Superintendent also monitors a bankrupt's compliance with the Act, Rules, and Directives. The Superintendent operates through an office in Ottawa, called the OSB: Office of the Superintendent of Bankruptcy.

SUPPORT ORDER: A support order is an order made under provincial *Family Law Act* legislation or the *Divorce Act* in favour of a spouse or the children of the marriage requiring the other spouse to make certain payments, lump sum and periodic.

TRANSFER AT UNDERVALUE: A transfer at undervalue is a transaction under the *Bankruptcy and Insolvency Act* whereby the bankrupt gave or received less than fair market value or no value for the goods or services within one to five years of bankruptcy. Where this occurs, the trustee can pursue the recovery of the property from the third party.

TRUSTEE IN BANKRUPTCY: The trustee in bankruptcy is a person or corporation who holds a licence from the OSB to administer bankrupt estates and proposals under the *Bankruptcy and Insolvency Act*.

WRIT OF SEIZURE AND SALE: This writ commands the sheriff following judgment to seize and sell the judgment debtor's assets for the judgment creditor. It is also called a writ of execution.

Appendix I
EXCERPTS FROM THE
BANKRUPTCY AND INSOLVENCY ACT

1. Definitions from Section 2

"bankrupt"

"bankrupt" means a person who has made an assignment or against whom a bankruptcy order has been made or the legal status of that person;

"debtor"

"debtor" includes an insolvent person and any person who, at the time an act of bankruptcy was committed by him or her, resided or carried on business in Canada and, where the context requires, includes a bankrupt;

"insolvent person"

"insolvent person" means a person who is not bankrupt and who resides or carries on business in Canada, whose liabilities to creditors provable as claims under this Act amount to $1,000, and

(a) who is for any reason unable to meet his or her obligations as they generally become due,

(b) who has ceased paying his or her current obligations in the ordinary course of business as they generally become due, or

(c) the aggregate of whose property is not, at a fair valuation, sufficient, or, if disposed of at a fairly conducted sale under legal process, would not be sufficient to enable payment of all his or her obligations, due and accruing due;

"property"

"property" means any type of property, whether situated in Canada or elsewhere, and includes money, goods, things in action, land and every description of property, whether real or personal, legal or equitable, as well as obligations, easements and every description of estate, interest and profit, present or future, vested or contingent, in, arising out of or incident to property;

"secured creditor"

"secured creditor" means a person holding a mortgage, hypothec, pledge, charge or lien on or against the property of the debtor or any part of that property as security for a debt due or accruing due to the person from the debtor, or a person whose claim is based on, or secured by, a negotiable instrument held as collateral security and on which the debtor is only indirectly or secondarily liable, and includes

(a) a person who has a right of retention or a prior claim constituting a real right, within the meaning of the *Civil Code of Quebec* or any other statute of the Province of Quebec, on or against the property of the debtor or any part of that property, or

(b) any of

(i) the vendor of any property sold to the debtor under a conditional or instalment sale,

(ii) the purchaser of any property from the debtor subject to a right of redemption, or

(iii) the trustee of a trust constituted by the debtor to secure the performance of an obligation,

if the exercise of the person's rights is subject to the provisions of Book Six of the *Civil Code of Quebec* entitled Prior Claims and Hypothecs that deal with the exercise of hypothecary rights; means a person holding a mortgage, hypothec, pledge, charge, lien or privilege on or against the property of the debtor or any part thereof as security for a debt due or accruing due to him or her from the debtor, or a person whose claim is based on, or secured by, a negotiable instrument held as collateral security and on which the debtor is only indirectly or secondarily liable

2. Acts of Bankruptcy from Section 42

Section 42. (1) A debtor commits an act of bankruptcy in each of the following cases:

(e) if the debtor permits any execution or other process issued against the debtor under which any of the debtor's property is seized, levied on or taken in execution to remain unsatisfied until within five days after the time fixed by the executing officer for the sale of the property or for 15 days after the seizure, levy or taking in execution, or if any of the debtor's property has been sold by the executing officer, or if the execution or other process has been held by the executing officer for a period of 15 days after written demand for payment without seizure, levy or taking in execution or satisfaction by payment, or if it is returned endorsed to the effect that the executing officer can find no property on which to levy or to seize or take, but if interpleader or opposition proceedings have been instituted with respect to the property seized, the time elapsing between the date at which the proceedings were instituted and the date at which the proceedings are finally disposed of, settled or abandoned shall not be taken into account in calculating the period of 15 days;

(f) if he or she exhibits to any meeting of his or her creditors any statement of his or her assets and liabilities that shows that he or she is insolvent, or presents or causes to be presented to any such meeting a written admission of his or her inability to pay his or her debts;

(g) if he or she assigns, removes, secretes or disposes of or attempts or is about to assign, remove, secrete or dispose of any of his or her property with intent to defraud, defeat or delay his or her creditors or any of them;

(h) if he or she gives notice to any of his or her creditors that he or she has suspended or that he or she is about to suspend payment of his or her debts;

(j) if he or she ceases to meet his or her liabilities generally as they become due.

3. Application for a Bankruptcy Order from Section 43

(1) Subject to this section, one or more creditors may file in court an application for a bankruptcy order against a debtor if it is alleged in the application that

(a) the debt or debts owing to the applicant creditor or creditors amount to $1,000; and

(b) the debtor has committed an act of bankruptcy within the six months preceding the filing of the application.

4. Assignment from Section 49

(1) An insolvent person or, if deceased, the executor or administrator of his or her estate or the liquidator of the succession, with the leave of the court, may make an assignment of all the insolvent person's property for the general benefit of the insolvent person's creditors.

(2) The assignment must be accompanied by a sworn statement in the prescribed form showing the debtor's property that is divisible among his or her creditors, the names and addresses of all his or her creditors and the amounts of their respective claims.

5. Property of the Bankrupt from Section 67

(Refer to Chapter 6)

Section 67. Property of bankrupt

(1) The property of a bankrupt divisible among his or her creditors shall not comprise

(a) property held by the bankrupt in trust for any other person;

(b) any property that as against the bankrupt is exempt from execution or seizure under any laws applicable in the province within which the property is situated and within which the bankrupt resides;

(b.1) goods and services tax credit payments that are made in prescribed circumstances to the bankrupt and that are not property referred to in paragraph (a) or (b);

(b.2) prescribed payments relating to the essential needs of an individual that are made in prescribed circumstances to the bankrupt and that are not property referred to in paragraph (a) or (b); or (b.3) without restricting the generality of paragraph (b), property in a registered retirement savings plan or a registered retirement income fund, as those expressions are defined in the *Income Tax Act*, or in any prescribed plan, other than property contributed to any such plan or fund in the 12 months before the date of bankruptcy, but it shall comprise

(c) all property wherever situated of the bankrupt at the date of the bankruptcy or that may be acquired by or devolve on the bankrupt before his or her discharge, including any refund owing to the bankrupt under the *Income Tax Act* in respect of the calendar year — or the fiscal year of the bankrupt if it is different from the calendar year — in which the bankrupt became a bankrupt, except the portion that

(i) is not subject to the operation of this Act, or

(ii) in the case of a bankrupt who is the judgment debtor named in a garnishee summons served on Her Majesty under the Family *Orders and Agreements Enforcement Assistance Act*, is garnishable money that is payable to the bankrupt and is to be paid under the garnishee summons, and

(d) such powers in or over or in respect of the property as might have been exercised by the bankrupt for his or her own benefit.

(2) Subject to subsection (3), notwithstanding any provision in federal or provincial legislation that has the effect of deeming property to be held in trust for Her Majesty, property of a bankrupt shall not be regarded as held in trust for Her Majesty for the purpose of paragraph (1)(a) unless it would be so regarded in the absence of that statutory provision.

(3) Subsection (2) does not apply in respect of amounts deemed to be held in trust under subsection 227(4) or (4.1) of the *Income Tax Act*, subsection 23(3) or (4) of the Canada Pension Plan or subsection 86(2) or (2.1) of the *Employment Insurance Act* (each of which is in this subsection referred to as a "federal provision") nor in respect of amounts deemed to be held in trust under any law of a province that creates a deemed trust the sole purpose of which is to ensure remittance to Her Majesty in right of the province of amounts deducted or withheld under a law of the province where

(a) that law of the province imposes a tax similar in nature to the tax imposed under the *Income Tax Act* and the amounts deducted or withheld under that law of the province are of the same nature as the amounts referred to in subsection 227(4) or (4.1) of the *Income Tax Act*, or

(b) the province is a "province providing a comprehensive pension plan" as defined in subsection 3(1) of the Canada Pension Plan, that law of the province establishes a "provincial pension plan" as defined in that subsection and the amounts deducted or withheld under that law of the province are of the same nature as amounts referred to in subsection 23(3) or (4) of the Canada Pension Plan, and for the purpose of this subsection, any provision of a law of a province that creates a deemed trust is, notwithstanding any Act of Canada or of a province or any other law, deemed to have the same effect and scope against any creditor, however secured, as the corresponding federal provision.

6. Consumer Proposal: Division II, Sections 66.11 – 66.40

(Refer to Chapter 10)

Definitions

Section 66.11

"administrator" means

(a) a trustee, or

(b) a person appointed or designated by the Superintendent to administer consumer proposals;

"consumer debtor"

means an individual who is bankrupt or insolvent whose aggregate debts, excluding any debts secured by the person's principal residence, are not more than $250,000 or any other prescribed amount;

"consumer proposal"

means a proposal made under this Division.

Section 66.12 Consumer proposal

(1) A consumer proposal may be made by a consumer debtor, subject to subsections (2) and 66.32(1).

Dealing with certain consumer proposals together

(1.1) Two or more consumer proposals may, in such circumstances as are specified in directives of the Superintendent, be dealt with as one consumer proposal where they could reasonably be dealt with together because of the financial relationship of the consumer debtors involved.

Restriction

(2) A consumer debtor who has filed a notice of intention or a proposal under Division I may not make a consumer proposal until the trustee appointed in respect of the notice of intention or proposal under Division I has been discharged.

To whom consumer proposal is made

(3) A consumer proposal shall be made to the creditors generally.

Creditors' response

(4) Any creditor may respond to a consumer proposal by filing with the administrator a proof of claim in the manner provided for in

(a) sections 124 to 126, in the case of unsecured creditors; or

(b) sections 124 to 134, in the case of secured creditors.

Term of consumer proposal

(5) A consumer proposal must provide that its performance is to be completed within five years.

Priority of claims, fees

(6) A consumer proposal must provide

(a) for the payment in priority to other claims of all claims directed to be so paid in the distribution of the property of the consumer debtor;

(b) for the payment of all prescribed fees and expenses

(i) of the administrator on and incidental to proceedings arising out of the consumer proposal, and

(ii) of any person in respect of counselling provided pursuant to paragraph 66.13(2)(b); and

(c) for the manner of distributing dividends.

Section 66.13. Commencement of proceedings

(1) A consumer debtor who wishes to make a consumer proposal shall commence proceedings by

(a) obtaining the assistance of an administrator in preparing the consumer proposal; and

(b) providing the administrator with the prescribed information on the consumer debtor's current financial situation.

Duties of administrator

(2) An administrator who agrees to assist a consumer debtor shall

(a) investigate, or cause to be investigated, the consumer debtor's property and financial affairs so as to be able to assess with reasonable accuracy the consumer debtor's financial situation and the cause of his or her insolvency;

(b) provide, or provide for, counselling in accordance with directives issued by the Superintendent pursuant to paragraph 5(4)(b);

(c) prepare a consumer proposal in the prescribed form; and

(d) subject to subsection (3), file with the Official Receiver a copy of the consumer proposal, signed by the consumer debtor, and the prescribed Statement of Affairs.

Where consumer proposal not to be filed

(3) The administrator shall not file a consumer proposal under paragraph (2)(d) if he or she has reason to believe that

(a) the debtor is not eligible to make a consumer proposal; or

(b) there has been non-compliance with anything required by this section or section 66.12.

Where consumer proposal wrongly filed

(4) Where the administrator determines, filing a consumer proposal under paragraph (2)(d), that it should not have been filed because the debtor was not eligible to make a consumer proposal, the administrator shall forthwith so inform the creditors and the Official Receiver, but the consumer proposal is not invalid by reason only that the debtor was not eligible to make the consumer proposal.

Duties of administrator

Section 66.14 The administrator shall, within ten days after filing a consumer proposal with the Official Receiver,

(a) prepare and file with the Official Receiver a report in the prescribed form setting out

(i) the results of the investigation made under paragraph 66.13(2)(a),

(ii) the administrator's opinion as to whether the consumer proposal is reasonable and fair to the consumer debtor and the creditors, and whether the consumer debtor will be able to perform it, and

(iv) a list of the creditors whose claims exceed $250; and

(b) send to every known creditor, in the prescribed form and manner,

(i) a copy of the consumer proposal and a copy of the Statement of Affairs referred to in paragraph 66.13(2)(d),

(ii) a copy of the report referred to in paragraph (a),

(iii) a form of proof of claim as prescribed, and

(iv) a statement explaining that a meeting of creditors will be called only if required under section 66.15 and that a review of the consumer proposal by a court will be made only if it is requested in accordance with subsection 66.22(1).

Section 66.15 Meeting of creditors

(1) The Official Receiver may, at any time within the 45-day period following the filing of the consumer proposal, direct the administrator to call a meeting of creditors.

Idem

(2) The administrator shall call a meeting of creditors

(a) forthwith after being so directed by the Official Receiver under subsection (1), or

(b) at the expiration of the 45-day period following the filing of the consumer proposal, if at that time creditors having in the aggregate at least 25 percent in value of the proven claims have so requested, and any meeting of creditors must be held within 21 days after being called.

Notice to be sent to creditors

(3) The administrator shall, at least ten days before a meeting called pursuant to this section, send to the consumer debtor, every known creditor and the Official Receiver, in the prescribed form and manner, a notice setting out

(a) the time and place of the meeting;

(b) a form of proxy as prescribed; and

(c) such other information and documentation as is prescribed.

Section 66.16 Chair of meeting

(1) The Official Receiver, or the nominee thereof, shall be the chair of a meeting called pursuant to section 66.15 and subsection 66.37(1) and shall decide any questions or disputes arising at the meeting, and any creditor may appeal any such decision to the court.

Adjournment of meeting for further investigation and examination

(2) Where the creditors by ordinary resolution at the meeting so require, the meeting shall be adjourned to such time and place as may be fixed by the chair

(a) to enable a further appraisal and investigation of the affairs and property of the consumer debtor to be made; or

(b) for the examination under oath of the consumer debtor or of such other person as may be believed to have knowledge of the affairs or property of the consumer debtor, and the testimony of the consumer debtor or such other person, if transcribed, shall be placed before the adjourned meeting or may be read in court on the application, if any, for the approval of the consumer proposal.

Section 66.17 Creditor may indicate assent or dissent

(1) Any creditor who has proved a claim may indicate assent to or dissent from the consumer proposal in the prescribed manner to the administrator at or prior to a meeting of creditors, or prior to the expiration of the 45-day period following the filing of the consumer proposal.

Effect of assent or dissent

(2) Unless it is rescinded, any dissent received by the administrator at or before a meeting of creditors has effect as if the creditor had been present and had voted at the meeting.

Section 66.18 Where consumer proposal deemed accepted

(1) Where, at the expiration of the 45-day period following the filing of the consumer proposal, no obligation has arisen under subsection 66.15(2) to call a meeting of creditors, the consumer proposal is deemed to be accepted by the creditors.

Idem

(2) Where there is no quorum at a meeting of creditors, the consumer proposal shall be deemed to be accepted by the creditors.

Section 66.19 Voting on consumer proposal

(1) At a meeting of creditors, the creditors may by ordinary resolution, voting all as one class, accept or refuse the consumer proposal as filed or as altered at the meeting or any adjournment thereof, subject to the rights of secured creditors.

Related creditor

(2) A creditor who is related to the consumer debtor may vote against but not for the acceptance of the consumer proposal.

Voting by administrator

(3) The administrator, as a creditor, may not vote on the consumer proposal.

Section 66.2 Creditors may provide for supervision of consumer debtor's affairs

The creditors, with the consent of the consumer debtor, may include such provisions or terms in the consumer proposal with respect to the supervision of the affairs of the consumer debtor as they may deem advisable.

Section 66.21 Appointment of inspectors

The creditors may appoint up to three inspectors of the estate of the consumer debtor, who shall have the powers of an inspector under this Act, subject to any extension or restriction of those powers by the terms of the consumer proposal.

Section 66.22 Application to court

(1) Where a consumer proposal is accepted or deemed accepted by the creditors, the administrator shall, if requested by the Official Receiver or any other interested party within 15 days after the day of acceptance or deemed acceptance, forthwith apply to the court to have the consumer proposal reviewed.

Where consumer proposal deemed approved by court

(2) Where, at the expiration of the 15th day after the day of acceptance or deemed acceptance of the consumer proposal by the creditors, no obligation has arisen under subsection (1) to apply to the court, the consumer proposal is deemed to be approved by the court.

Section 66.23 Procedure for application to court

Where the administrator applies to the court pursuant to subsection 66.22(1), the administrator shall

(a) send a notice of the hearing of the application, in the prescribed manner and at least 15 days before the date of the hearing, to the consumer debtor, to every creditor who has proved a claim and to the Official Receiver;

(b) forward a copy of the report referred to in paragraph (c) to the Official Receiver at least ten days before the date of the hearing; and

(c) at least two days before the date of the hearing, file with the court a report in the prescribed form on the consumer proposal and the conduct of the consumer debtor.

Section 66.24 Court to hear report of administrator, etc.

(1) The court shall, before approving the consumer proposal, hear the report mentioned in paragraph 66.23(c) and, in addition, shall hear the Official Receiver, the administrator, the consumer debtor, any opposing, objecting or dissenting creditor or other interested party, and such further evidence as the court may require.

Refusal to approve the consumer proposal

(2) Where the court is of the opinion that the terms of the consumer proposal are not reasonable or are not fair to the consumer debtor and the creditors, the court shall refuse to approve the consumer proposal, and the court may refuse to approve the consumer proposal whenever it is established that the consumer debtor

(a) has committed any one of the offences mentioned in sections 198 to 200; or

(b) was not eligible to make a consumer proposal when the consumer proposal was filed with the Official Receiver.

Proposal must comply with Act

(3) The court shall refuse to approve a consumer proposal if it does not comply with subsections 66.12(5) and (6).

Power of court

(4) Subject to subsections (1) to (3), the court may either approve or refuse to approve the consumer proposal.

Section 66.25 Withdrawal of consumer proposal

A consumer debtor may withdraw a consumer proposal

(a) at any time before its deemed approval by the court by virtue of subsection 66.22(2), where no court review is requested; or

(b) where a court review is requested, at any time before its actual approval or refusal by the court pursuant to section 66.24.

Section 66.251 Where periodic payments not provided for

Where a proposal is approved or deemed approved by the court and the terms of the proposal do not provide for the distribution of available monies at least once every three months, the administrator shall forthwith, upon ascertaining any change in the consumer debtor's circumstances that leads the administrator to conclude, after consultation with the debtor where practicable, that such change could jeopardize the consumer debtor's ability to meet the terms of the proposal, in writing, notify the Official Receiver and every known creditor of the change.

Section 66.26 Payments to administrator

(1) All monies payable under the consumer proposal shall be paid to the administrator and, after payment of all fees and expenses mentioned in paragraph 66.12(6)(b), the administrator shall distribute available monies to the creditors in accordance with the terms of the consumer proposal.

Deposit of monies

(2) In such circumstances as are specified in directives of the Superintendent and with the approval of the Superintendent, the administrator may deposit all monies relating to the administration of consumer proposals in a single trust account.

Section 147 applies

(3) Section 147 applies, with such modifications as the circumstances require, to all distributions made to the creditors by the administrator pursuant to subsection (1).

Section 66.27 Notifications

The administrator shall, within five days after

(a) the refusal of a consumer proposal by the creditors,

(b) the refusal of a consumer proposal by the court, and

(c) the withdrawal of a consumer proposal by the consumer debtor, so notify in the prescribed form and manner the consumer debtor, every known creditor and the Official Receiver.

Section 66.28 Time for determining claims

(1) The time with respect to which the claims of creditors shall be determined is the time of the filing of the consumer proposal.

On whom approval binding

(2) Subject to subsection (2.1), a consumer proposal accepted, or deemed accepted, by the creditors and approved, or deemed approved, by the court is binding on creditors in respect of

(a) all unsecured claims, and

(b) secured claims for which proofs of claim have been filed in the manner provided for in sections 124 to 134.

When consumer debtor is released from debt

(2.1) A consumer proposal accepted, or deemed accepted by the creditors and approved, or deemed approved, by the court does not release the consumer debtor from any particular debt or liability referred to in subsection 178(1) unless the consumer proposal explicitly provides for the compromise of that debt or liability and the creditor in relation to that debt or liability voted for the acceptance of the consumer proposal.

Certain persons not released

(3) The acceptance of a consumer proposal by a creditor does not release any person who would not be released under this Act by the discharge of the consumer debtor.

Section 66.29 Administrator may issue certificate

(1) If a consumer proposal is approved or deemed approved by the court, the administrator may, if the administrator believes on reasonable grounds that the debtor owns land or other valuable property, issue a certificate in respect of the proposal, and may cause the certificate to be filed in any place where a certificate of judgment, writ of seizure and sale or other like document may be filed or where a legal hypothec of judgment creditors may be registered.

Effect of filing certificate

(2) A certificate filed under subsection (1) operates as a certificate of judgment, writ of execution or legal hypothec of judgment creditors until the proposal is fully performed.

Section 66.3 Annulment of consumer proposal

(1) Where default is made in the performance of any provision in a consumer proposal, or where it appears to the court

(a) that the debtor was not eligible to make a consumer proposal when the consumer proposal was filed,

(b) that the consumer proposal cannot continue without injustice or undue delay, or

(c) that the approval of the court was obtained by fraud, the court may, on application, with such notice as the court may direct to the consumer debtor and, if applicable, to the administrator and to the creditors, annul the consumer proposal.

Validity of things done

(2) An order made under subsection (1) shall be made without prejudice to the validity of any sale, disposition of property or payment duly made, or anything duly done under or in pursuance of the consumer proposal, and notwithstanding the annulment of the consumer proposal, a guarantee given pursuant to the consumer proposal remains in full force and effect in accordance with its terms.

Annulment for offence

(3) A consumer proposal, although accepted or approved, may be annulled by order of the court at the request of the administrator or of any creditor whenever the consumer debtor is afterwards convicted of any offence under this Act.

Notification of annulment

(4) Where an order annulling the consumer proposal of a consumer debtor who is not a bankrupt has been made pursuant to this section, the administrator shall forthwith so inform the creditors and file a report thereof in the prescribed form with the Official Receiver.

Annulment effect

(5) Where a consumer proposal made by a bankrupt is annulled,

(a) the consumer debtor is deemed on the annulment to have made an assignment and the order annulling the proposal shall so state;

(b) the trustee who is the administrator of the proposal shall, within five days after the order is made, send notice of the meeting of creditors under section 102, at which meeting the creditors may by ordinary resolution, notwithstanding section 14, affirm the appointment of the trustee or appoint another trustee in lieu of that trustee; and

(c) the trustee shall forthwith file a report thereof in the prescribed form with the Official Receiver, who shall thereupon issue a certificate of assignment in the prescribed form, which has the same effect for the purposes of this Act as an assignment filed pursuant to section 49.

Section 66.31 Deemed annulment — default of payment

(1) Unless the court has previously ordered otherwise or unless an amendment to the consumer proposal has previously been filed, a consumer proposal is deemed to be annuled on

(a) in the case when payments under the consumer proposal are to be made monthly or more frequently, the day on which the consumer debtor is in default for an amount that is equal to or more than the amount of three payments; or

(b) in the case when payments under the consumer proposal are to be made less frequently than monthly, the day that is three months after the day on which the consumer debtor is in default in respect of any payment.

Deemed annulment — amendment withdrawn or refused

(2) If an amendment to a consumer proposal filed before the deemed annulment of the consumer proposal under subsection (1) is withdrawn or refused by the creditors or the court, the consumer proposal is deemed to be annulled at the time that the amendment is withdrawn or refused.

Duties of administrator in relation to deemed assignment

(3) Without delay after a consumer proposal is deemed to be annulled, the administrator shall

(a) file with the Official Receiver a report in the prescribed form in relation to the deemed annulment; and

(b) send a notice to the creditors informing them of the deemed annulment.

Effects of deemed annulment — consumer proposal by a bankrupt

(4) If a consumer proposal made by a bankrupt is deemed to be annulled,

(a) the consumer debtor is deemed to have made an assignment on the day on which the consumer proposal is deemed to be annulled;

(b) the trustee who is the administrator of the consumer proposal shall, within five days after the day on which the consumer proposal is deemed to be annulled, send notice of the meeting of creditors under section 102, at which meeting the creditors may by ordinary resolution, despite section 14, affirm the appointment of the trustee or appoint another trustee in lieu of that trustee; and

(c) the trustee shall, without delay, file with the Official Receiver, in the prescribed form, a report of the deemed annulment and the Official Receiver shall, without delay, issue a certificate of assignment, in the prescribed form, which has the same effect for the purposes of this Act as an assignment filed under section 49.

Validity of things done before deemed assignment

(5) A deemed annulment of a consumer proposal does not prejudice the validity of any sale or disposition of property or payment duly made, or anything duly done under or in pursuance of the consumer proposal and, despite the deemed annulment, a guarantee given under the consumer proposal remains in full force and effect in accordance with its terms.

Notice of possibility of consumer proposal being automatically revived

(6) In the case of a deemed annulment of a consumer proposal made by a person other than a bankrupt, if the administrator considers it appropriate to do so in the circumstances, he or she may, with notice to the Official Receiver, send to the creditors — within 30 days, or any other number of days that is prescribed, after the day on which the consumer proposal was deemed to be annulled — a notice in the prescribed form informing them that the consumer proposal will be automatically revived 60 days, or any other number of days that is prescribed, after the day on which it was deemed to be annulled unless one of them files with the administrator, in the prescribed manner, a notice of objection to the revival.

Automatic revival

(7) If the notice is sent by the administrator and no notice of objection is filed during the period referred to in subsection (6), the consumer proposal is automatically revived on the expiry of that period.

Notice of no automatic revival

(8) If a notice of objection is filed during the period referred to in subsection (6), the administrator is to send, without delay, to the Official Receiver and to each creditor a notice in the prescribed form informing them that the consumer proposal is not going to be automatically revived on the expiry of that period.

Administrator may apply to court to revive consumer proposal

(9) The administrator may at any time apply to the court, with notice to the Official Receiver and the creditors, for an order reviving any consumer proposal of a consumer debtor who is not a bankrupt that was deemed to be annulled, and the court, if it considers it appropriate to do so in the circumstances, may make an order reviving the consumer proposal, on any terms that the court considers appropriate.

Duty of administrator if consumer proposal is revived

(10) Without delay after a consumer proposal is revived, the administrator shall

(a) file with the Official Receiver a report in the prescribed form in relation to the revival; and

(b) send a notice to the creditors informing them of the revival.

Validity of things done before revival

(11) The revival of a consumer proposal does not prejudice the validity of anything duly done — between the day on which the consumer proposal is deemed to be annulled and the day on which it is revived — by a creditor in the exercise of any rights revived by subsection 66.32(2).

Section 66.32 Effects of annulment

(1) Unless the court otherwise orders, where a consumer proposal is annulled or deemed annulled, the consumer debtor

(a) may not make another consumer proposal, and

(b) is not entitled to any relief provided by sections 69 to 69.2 until all claims for which proofs of claim were filed and accepted are either paid in full or are extinguished by the operation of subsection 178(2).

Idem

(2) Where a consumer proposal is annulled or deemed annulled, the rights of the creditors are revived for the amount of their claims less any dividends received.

Section 66.34 Certain rights limited

(1) If a consumer proposal has been filed in respect of a consumer debtor, no person may terminate or amend any agreement, including a security agreement, with the consumer debtor, or claim an accelerated payment, or the forfeiture of the term, under any

agreement, including a security agreement with the consumer debtor, by reason only that

> (a) the consumer debtor is insolvent, or

> (b) a consumer proposal has been filed in respect of the consumer debtor until the consumer proposal has been withdrawn, refused by the creditors or the court, annulled or deemed annulled.

Idem

(2) Where the agreement referred to in subsection (1) is a lease, subsection (1) shall be read as including the following paragraph:

> (c) "the consumer debtor has not paid rent in respect of a period preceding the filing of the consumer proposal."

Idem

(3) Where a consumer proposal has been filed in respect of a consumer debtor, no public utility may discontinue service to that consumer debtor by reason only that

> (a) the consumer debtor is insolvent,

> (b) a consumer proposal has been filed in respect of the consumer debtor, or

> (c) the consumer debtor has not paid for services rendered, or material provided, before the filing of the consumer proposal until the consumer proposal has been withdrawn, refused by the creditors or the court, annulled or deemed annulled.

Certain acts not prevented

(4) Nothing in subsections (1) to (3) shall be construed

> (a) as prohibiting a person from requiring payments to be made in cash for goods, services, use of leased property or other valuable consideration provided after the filing of the consumer proposal; or

> (b) as requiring the further advance of money or credit.

Provisions of section override agreement

(5) Any provision in an agreement that has the effect of providing for, or permitting, anything that, in substance, is contrary to subsections (1) to (3) is of no force or effect.

Powers of court

(6) The court may, on application by a party to an agreement or by a public utility, declare that this section does not apply, or applies

only to the extent declared by the court, where the applicant satisfies the court that the operation of this section would likely cause it significant financial hardship.

Eligible financial contracts

(7) Subsection (1) does not apply in respect of an eligible financial contract.

Permitted actions

(8) Despite section 69.2, the following actions are permitted in respect of an eligible financial contract that is entered into before the filing of a consumer proposal and is terminated on or after that filing, but only in accordance with the provisions of that contract:

>(a) the netting or setting off or compensation of obligations between the consumer debtor and the other parties to the eligible financial contract; and

>(b) any dealing with financial collateral including

>>(i) the sale or foreclosure or, in the Province of Quebec, the surrender of financial collateral, and

>>(ii) the setting off or compensation of financial collateral or the application of the proceeds or value of financial collateral.

Net termination values

(9) If net termination values determined in accordance with an eligible financial contract referred to in subsection (8) are owed by the consumer debtor to another party to the eligible financial contract, that other party is deemed, for the purposes of subsection 69.2(1), to be a creditor of the consumer debtor with a claim provable in bankruptcy in respect of those net termination values.

Section 66.35 Assignment of wages

>(1) An assignment of existing or future wages made by a consumer debtor before the filing of a consumer proposal is of no effect in respect of wages earned after the filing of the consumer proposal.

Assignment of debts at request of administrator

>(2) In order to ensure compliance with the terms of a consumer proposal, the administrator may, at any time after the consumer proposal is filed, require of, and take from, the consumer debtor an assignment of any amount payable to the consumer debtor, including wages, that may become payable in the future, but no

such assignment can, unless the consumer debtor agrees, be for an amount greater than is due and payable pursuant to the terms of the consumer proposal.

Third parties protected

(3) An assignment made pursuant to subsection (2) is of no effect against a person owing the amount payable until a notice of the assignment is served on that person.

When section ceases to apply

(4) This section ceases to apply where the consumer proposal is refused by the creditors or by the court, or is withdrawn, annulled or deemed annulled.

Section 66.36 No dismissal, etc., of employee

No employer shall dismiss, suspend, lay off or otherwise discipline a consumer debtor on the sole ground that a consumer proposal has been filed in respect of that consumer debtor.

Section 66.37 Amendment to consumer proposal

If an administrator files an amendment to a consumer proposal before the withdrawal, refusal, approval or deemed approval by the court of the consumer proposal, or after the approval or deemed approval by the court of the consumer proposal and before it has been fully performed or annulled or deemed annulled, the provisions of this Division apply to the consumer proposal and the amended consumer proposal, with any modifications that the circumstances require, and, for that purpose, the definition "consumer debtor" in section 66.11 is to be read as follows:

"consumer debtor" means an individual who is insolvent;

Section 66.38 Certificate where consumer proposal performed

(1) If a consumer proposal is fully performed, the administrator shall issue a certificate to that effect, in the prescribed form, to the consumer debtor and to the Official Receiver.

(2) Subsection (1) does not apply in respect of a consumer debtor who has refused or neglected to receive counselling provided under paragraph 66.13(2)(b).

Section 66.39 Administrator's accounts, discharge

The form and content of the administrator's accounts, the procedure for the preparation and taxation of those accounts and the procedure for the discharge of the administrator shall be as prescribed.

Section 66.4 Act to apply

(1) All the provisions of this Act, except Division I of this Part, in so far as they are applicable, apply, with such modifications as the circumstances require, to consumer proposals.

Where consumer debtor is bankrupt

(2) Where a consumer proposal is made by a consumer debtor who is a bankrupt,

(a) the consumer proposal must be approved by the inspectors, if any, before any further action is taken thereon;

(b) the consumer debtor must have obtained the assistance of a trustee who shall act as administrator of the proposal in the preparation and execution thereof;

(c) the time with respect to which the claims of creditors shall be determined is the time at which the consumer debtor became bankrupt; and

(d) the approval or deemed approval by the court of the consumer proposal operates to annul the bankruptcy and to revest in the consumer debtor, or in such other person as the court may approve, all the right, title and interest of the trustee in the property of the consumer debtor, unless the terms of the consumer proposal otherwise provide.

7. Attachment of Wages from Section 68

Section 68 Directives regarding surplus income

(1) The Superintendent shall, by directive, establish in respect of the provinces or one or more bankruptcy districts or parts of bankruptcy districts, the standards for determining the surplus income of an individual bankrupt and the amount that a bankrupt who has surplus income is required to pay to the estate of the bankrupt.

Definitions

(2) The following definitions apply in this section.

"surplus income" means the portion of a bankrupt individual's total income that exceeds that which is necessary to enable the bankrupt individual to maintain a reasonable standard of living, having regard to the applicable standards established under subsection (1).

"total income"

(a) includes, despite paragraphs 67(1)(b) and (b.3), a bankrupt's revenues of whatever nature or from whatever source that are earned or received by the bankrupt between the date of the bankruptcy and the date of the bankrupt's discharge, including those received as damages for wrongful dismissal, received as a pay equity settlement or received under an Act of Parliament, or of the legislature of a province, that relates to workers' compensation; but

(b) does not include any amounts received by the bankrupt between the date of the bankruptcy and the date of the bankrupt's discharge, as a gift, a legacy or an inheritance or as any other windfall.

Determination of trustee re surplus income

(3) The trustee shall, having regard to the applicable standards and to the personal and family situation of the bankrupt, determine whether the bankrupt has surplus income. The determination must also be made

(a) whenever the trustee becomes aware of a material change in the bankrupt's financial situation; and

(b) whenever the trustee is required to prepare a report referred to in subsection 170(1).

Duties of trustee relating to determination

(4) Whenever the trustee is required to determine whether the bankrupt has surplus income, the trustee shall

(a) if the trustee determines that there is surplus income,

(i) fix, having regard to the applicable standards, the amount that the bankrupt is required to pay to the estate of the bankrupt,

(ii) inform, in the prescribed manner, the Official Receiver, and every creditor who has requested such information, of the amount fixed under subparagraph (i), and

(iii) take reasonable measures to ensure that the bankrupt complies with the requirement to pay; and

(b) if the trustee determines that there is no surplus income, inform, in the prescribed manner, the Official Receiver, and every creditor who has requested such information, of that determination.

Official Receiver recommendation

(5) If the Official Receiver determines that the amount required to be paid by the bankrupt is substantially not in accordance with the applicable standards, the Official Receiver shall recommend to the trustee and to the bankrupt an amount required to be paid that the Official Receiver determines is in accordance with the applicable standards.

Trustee may fix another amount

(5.1) On receipt of the Official Receiver's recommendation, the trustee may fix, having regard to the applicable standards, another amount as the amount that the bankrupt is required to pay to the estate of the bankrupt, and if the trustee does so, the trustee shall

(a) inform the Official Receiver and every creditor, in the prescribed manner, of the amount fixed under this subsection; and

(b) take reasonable measures to ensure that the bankrupt complies with the requirement to pay.

Trustee may request mediation

(6) If the trustee and the bankrupt are not in agreement with the amount that the bankrupt is required to pay under subsection (4) or (5.1), the trustee shall, without delay, in the prescribed form, send to the Official Receiver a request that the matter be determined by mediation and send a copy of the request to the bankrupt.

Creditors may request mediation

(7) On a creditor's request made within 30 days after the day on which the trustee informed the creditor of the amount fixed under subsection (4) or (5.1), the trustee shall, within 5 days after the day on which the 30-day period ends, send to the Official Receiver a request, in the prescribed form, that the matter of the amount that the bankrupt is required to pay be determined by mediation and send a copy of the request to the bankrupt and the creditor.

Mediation procedure

(8) A mediation shall be in accordance with prescribed procedures.

File

(9) Documents contained in a file on the mediation of a matter under this section form part of the records referred to in subsection 11.1(2).

Application to court to fix amount

(10) The trustee may, in any of the following circumstances — and shall apply if requested to do so by the Official Receiver in the circumstances referred to in paragraph (a) — apply to the court to fix, by order, in accordance with the applicable standards, and having regard to the personal and family situation of the bankrupt, the amount that the bankrupt is required to pay to the estate of the bankrupt:

(a) if the trustee has not implemented a recommendation made by the Official Receiver under subsection (5);

(b) if the matter submitted to mediation has not been resolved by the mediation; or

(c) if the bankrupt has failed to comply with the requirement to pay as determined under this section.

Fixing fair and reasonable remuneration in the case of related persons

(11) The court may fix an amount that is fair and reasonable

(a) as salary, wages or other remuneration for the services being performed by a bankrupt for a person employing the bankrupt, or

(b) as payment for or commission in respect of any services being performed by a bankrupt for a person, where the person is related to the bankrupt, and the court may, by order, determine the part of the salary, wages or other remuneration, or the part of the payment or commission, that shall be paid to the trustee on the basis of the amount so fixed by the court, unless it appears to the court that the services have been performed for the benefit of the bankrupt and are not of any substantial benefit to the person for whom they were performed.

Modification of order

(12) On the application of any interested person, the court may, at any time, amend an order made under this section to take into account material changes that have occurred in the financial situation of the bankrupt.

Default by other person

(13) An order of the court made under this section may be served on a person from whom the bankrupt is entitled to receive money and, in such case,

> (a) the order binds the person to pay to the estate of the bankrupt the amount fixed by the order; and

> (b) if the person fails to comply with the terms of the order, the court may, on the application of the trustee, order the person to pay the trustee the amount of money that the estate of the bankrupt would have received had the person complied with the terms of the order.

Application is a proceeding

(14) For the purposes of section 38, an application referred to in subsection (10) is deemed to be a proceeding for the benefit of the estate.

Property included for enforcement purposes

(15) For the purpose of this section, a requirement that a bankrupt pay an amount to the estate is enforceable against the bankrupt's total income.

When obligations to pay ceases

(16) If an opposition to the automatic discharge of a bankrupt individual who is required to pay an amount to the estate is filed, the bankrupt's obligation under this section ceases on the day on which the bankrupt would have been automatically discharged had the opposition not been filed, but nothing in this subsection precludes the court from determining that the bankrupt is required to pay to the estate an amount that the court considers appropriate.

Section 68.1 Assignment of wages

(1) An assignment of existing or future wages made by a debtor before the debtor became bankrupt is of no effect in respect of wages earned after the bankruptcy.

Assignment of book debts

(2) An assignment of existing or future amounts receivable as payment for or commission or professional fees in respect of services rendered by a debtor who is an individual before the debtor became bankrupt is of no effect in respect of such amounts earned or generated after the bankruptcy.

8. Duties of the Bankrupt from Sections 158 – 159

(Refer to Chapter 8)

Section 158. Duties of bankrupt

A bankrupt shall

(a) make discovery of and deliver all his or her property that is under his or her possession or control to the trustee or to any person authorized by the trustee to take possession of it or any part thereof;

(a.1) in such circumstances as are specified in directives of the Superintendent, deliver to the trustee, for cancellation, all credit cards issued to and in the possession or control of the bankrupt;

(b) deliver to the trustee all books, records, documents, writings and papers including, without restricting the generality of the foregoing, title papers, insurance policies and tax records and returns and copies thereof in any way relating to his or her property or affairs;

(c) at such time and place as may be fixed by the Official Receiver, attend before the Official Receiver or before any other Official Receiver delegated by the Official Receiver for examination under oath with respect to his or her conduct, the causes of his or her bankruptcy and the disposition of his or her property;

(d) within seven days following his or her bankruptcy, unless the time is extended by the Official Receiver, prepare and submit to the trustee in quadruplicate a statement of his or her affairs in the prescribed form verified by affidavit and showing the particulars of his or her assets and liabilities, the names and addresses of his or her creditors, the securities held by them respectively, the dates when the securities were respectively given and such further or other information as may be required, but where the affairs of the bankrupt are so involved or complicated that he or she cannot himself or herself reasonably prepare a proper statement of his or her affairs, the Official Receiver may, as an expense of the administration of the estate, authorize the employment of a qualified person to assist in the preparation of the statement;

(e) make or give all the assistance within his or her power to the trustee in making an inventory of his or her assets;

(f) make disclosure to the trustee of all property disposed of within one year preceding his or her bankruptcy, or for such further antecedent period as the court may direct, and how and to whom and for what consideration any part thereof was disposed of except such part as had been disposed of in the ordinary manner of trade or used for reasonable personal expenses;

(g) make disclosure to the trustee of all property disposed of by gift or settlement without adequate valuable consideration within five years preceding his or her bankruptcy;

(h) attend the first meeting of his or her creditors unless prevented by sickness or other sufficient cause and submit thereat to examination;

(i) when required, attend other meetings of his or her creditors or of the inspectors, or attend on the trustee;

(j) submit to such other examinations under oath with respect to his or her property or affairs as required;

(k) aid to the utmost of his or her power in the realization of his or her property and the distribution of the proceeds among his or her creditors;

(l) execute such powers of attorney, conveyances, deeds and instruments as may be required;

(m) examine the correctness of all proofs of claims filed, if required by the trustee;

(n) in case any person has to his or her knowledge filed a false claim, disclose the fact immediately to the trustee;

(o) generally do all such acts and things in relation to his or her property and the distribution of the proceeds among his or her creditors as may be reasonably required by the trustee, or may be prescribed by the General Rules, or may be directed by the court by any special order made with reference to any particular case or made on the occasion of any special application by the trustee, or any creditor or person interested; and

(p) until his or her application for discharge has been disposed of and the administration of the estate completed, keep the trustee advised at all times of his or her place of residence or address.

Section 159 Where bankrupt is a corporation

Section 159. Where a bankrupt is a corporation, the officer executing the assignment, or such

(a) officer of the corporation, or

(b) person who has, or has had, directly or indirectly, control in fact of the corporation as the Official Receiver may specify, shall attend before the Official Receiver for examination and shall perform all of the duties imposed on a bankrupt by section 158, and, in case of failure to do so, the officer or person is punishable as though that officer or person were the bankrupt.

9. Examination of the Bankrupt from Section 163

(1) The trustee, on ordinary resolution passed by the creditors or on the written request or resolution of a majority of the inspectors, may, without an order, examine under oath before the registrar of the court or other authorized person, the bankrupt, any person reasonably thought to have knowledge of the affairs of the bankrupt or any person who is or has been an agent or mandatary, or a clerk, a servant, an officer, a director or an employee of the bankrupt, respecting the bankrupt or the bankrupt's dealings or property and may order any person liable to be so examined to produce any books, documents, correspondence or papers in that person's possession or power relating in all or in part to the bankrupt or the bankrupt's dealings or property.

10. Debts Not Released by Discharge from Section 178

(Refer to Chapter 7)

Section 178 Debts not released by order of discharge

(1) An order of discharge does not release the bankrupt from

(a) any fine, penalty, restitution order or other order similar in nature to a fine, penalty or restitution order, imposed by a court in respect of an offence, or any debt arising out of a recognizance or bail;

(a.1) any award of damages by a court in civil proceedings in respect of

(i) bodily harm intentionally inflicted, or sexual assault, or

(ii) wrongful death resulting therefrom;

(b) any debt or liability for alimony or alimentary pension;

(c) any debt or liability arising under a judicial decision establishing affiliation or respecting support or maintenance, or under an agreement for maintenance and support of a spouse, former spouse, former common-law partner or child living apart from the bankrupt;

(d) any debt or liability arising out of fraud, embezzlement, misappropriation or defalcation while acting in a fiduciary capacity or, in the Province of Quebec, as a trustee or administrator of the property of others;

(e) any debt or liability resulting from obtaining property or services by false pretences or fraudulent misrepresentation, other than a debt or liability that arises from an equity claim;

(f) liability for the dividend that a creditor would have been entitled to receive on any provable claim not disclosed to the trustee, unless the creditor had notice or knowledge of the bankruptcy and failed to take reasonable action to prove his or her claim.

(g) any debt or obligation in respect of a loan made under the *Canada Student Loans Act*, the *Canada Student Financial Assistance Act* or any enactment of a province that provides for loans or guarantees of loans to students where the date of bankruptcy of the bankrupt occurred

(i) before the date on which the bankrupt ceased to be a full- or part-time student, as the case may be, under the applicable Act or enactment, or

(ii) within seven years after the date on which the bankrupt ceased to be a full- or part-time student.

(h) any debt for interest owed in relation to an amount referred to in any of the paragraphs (a) to (g).

Claims released

(2) Subject to subsection (1), an order of discharge releases the bankrupt from all claims provable in bankruptcy.

11. Bankruptcy Offences from Sections 198 – 201

Section 198 Bankruptcy offences

Any bankrupt who

(a) fails, without reasonable cause, to do any of the things required of him or her under section 158,

(b) makes any fraudulent disposition of his or her property before or after bankruptcy,

(c) refuses or neglects to answer fully and truthfully all proper questions put to him or her at any examination held pursuant to this Act,

(d) makes a false entry or knowingly makes a material omission in a statement or an accounting,

(e) after or within the 12 months immediately preceding his or her bankruptcy, conceals, destroys, mutilates, falsifies, makes an omission in or disposes of, or is privy to the concealment, destruction, mutilation, falsification, omission from or disposition of, a book or document affecting or relating to his or her property or affairs, unless he or she proves that he or she had no intent to conceal the state of his or her affairs,

(f) after or within the 12 months immediately preceding his or her bankruptcy, obtains any credit or any property by false representations made by him or her or made by any other person to his or her knowledge,

(g) after or within the 12 months immediately preceding his or her bankruptcy, fraudulently conceals or removes any property of a value of $50 or more or any debt due to or from him or her, or

(h) after or within the 12 months immediately preceding his or her bankruptcy, pawns, pledges or disposes of any property that he or she has obtained on credit and has not paid for, unless in the case of a trader the pawning, pledging or disposing is in the ordinary way of trade and unless in any case he or she proves that he or she had no intent to defraud, is guilty of an offence punishable on summary conviction and is liable to a fine not exceeding $5,000 or to imprisonment for a term not exceeding one year or to both, or is guilty of an indictable offence and is liable to a fine not exceeding $10,000 or to imprisonment for a term not exceeding three years or to both.

Section 199 Failure to disclose fact of being undischarged

An undischarged bankrupt who

(a) engages in any trade or business without disclosing to all persons with whom the undischarged bankrupt enters into any business transaction that the undischarged bankrupt is an undischarged bankrupt, or

(b) obtains credit to a total of $1,000 or more from any person or persons without informing such persons that the undischarged bankrupt is an undischarged bankrupt, is guilty of an offence punishable on summary conviction and is liable to a fine not exceeding $5,000 or to imprisonment for a term not exceeding one year, or to both.

Section 200 Bankrupt failing to keep proper books of account

(1) Any person becoming bankrupt or making a proposal who has on any previous occasion been bankrupt or made a proposal to the person's creditors is guilty of an offence punishable on summary conviction and is liable to a fine not exceeding $5,000 or to imprisonment for a term not exceeding one year, or to both, if

(a) being engaged in any trade or business, at any time during the two years immediately preceding his or her bankruptcy, that person has not kept and preserved proper books of account; or

(b) after or within the two-year period mentioned in paragraph (a), that person conceals, destroys, mutilates, falsifies or disposes of, or is privy to the concealment, destruction, mutilation, falsification or disposition of, any book or document affecting or relating to his or her property or affairs, unless he or she proves that he or she had no intent to conceal the state of his or her affairs.

Proper books of account defined

(2) For the purposes of this section, a debtor shall be deemed not to have kept proper books of account if he or she has not kept such books or accounts as are necessary to exhibit or explain his or her transactions and financial position in his or her trade or business, including a book or books containing entries from day to day in sufficient detail of all cash received and cash paid, and, where the trade or business has involved dealings in goods, also accounts of all goods sold and purchased, and statements of annual and other stock-takings.

Section 201 False claim, etc.

(1) Where a creditor, or a person claiming to be a creditor, in any proceedings under this Act, wilfully and with intent to defraud makes any false claim or any proof, declaration or statement of account that is untrue in any material particular, the creditor or person is guilty of an offence punishable on summary conviction and is liable

to a fine not exceeding $5,000, or to imprisonment for a term not exceeding one year, or to both.

Unlawful transactions

(3) Where the bankrupt enters into any transaction with any person for the purpose of obtaining a benefit or advantage to which either of them would not be entitled, the bankrupt is guilty of an offence punishable on summary conviction and is liable to a fine not exceeding $5,000, or to imprisonment for a term not exceeding one year, or to both.

12. Support Creditors from Sections 136 and 178

Section 136(1) Scheme of distribution

136. (1) Subject to the rights of secured creditors, the proceeds realized from the property of a bankrupt shall be applied in priority of payment as follows:

(d.1) claims in respect of debts or liabilities referred to in paragraph 178(1)(b) [alimony] or (c) [support], if provable by virtue of subsection 121(4), for periodic amounts accrued in the year before the date of the bankruptcy that are payable, plus any lump sum amount that is payable;

Section 178 Debts not released by order of discharge

(1) An order of discharge does not release the bankrupt from

(b) any debt or liability for alimony or alimentary pension;

(c) any debt or liability arising under a judicial decision establishing affiliation or respecting support or maintenance, or under an agreement for maintenance and support of a spouse, former spouse, former common-law partner or child living apart from the bankrupt.

Appendix 2
ADDITIONAL READING AND CONTACT INFORMATION

1. Additional Reading

There are many sources of good reading on consumer bankruptcies and consumer proposals.

Industry Canada, on behalf of the federal government, publishes a booklet called "Dealing with Debt: A Consumer's Guide to Bankruptcy."

The Office of the Superintendent of Bankruptcy publishes newsletters from time to time referring to articles and booklets on mediation, insolvency statistics, criminal prosecutions, and publications for young people from those in kindergarten to those attending postsecondary schools, on what they should know about financial affairs.

CCH Canadian Limited in Toronto published in 2001 my companion book for businesses called *Bennett's A–Z Guide to Bankruptcy: A Professional's Handbook*.

Many trustees in bankruptcy have their own websites which may contain information about the bankruptcy process.

2. Contact Information

2.1 The Superintendent of Bankruptcy

Heritage Place
155 Queen Street, 4th Floor
Ottawa, Ontario K1A 0H5
Tel.: 613-941-1000
Fax: 613-941-2862
www.ic.gc.ca/eic/site/bsf-osb.nsf/eng/home

2.2 The Offices of Official Receivers

Alberta

Standard Life Tower
639 5th Avenue SW, Suite 400
Calgary, Alberta T2P 0M9
Tel.: 1-877-376-9902 (toll free)
Fax: 403-292-5188

Canada Place Building
9700 Jasper Avenue NW, Suite 725
Edmonton, Alberta T5J 4C3
Tel.: 1-877-376-9902 (toll free)
Fax: 780-495-2466

British Columbia and Yukon

300 Georgia Street W, Suite 2000
Vancouver, British Columbia V6B 6E1
Tel.: 1-877-376-9902 (toll free)
Fax: 604-666-4610

Manitoba

400 St. Mary Avenue, 4th Floor
Winnipeg, Manitoba R3C 4K5
Tel.: 1-877-376-9902 (toll free)
Fax: 204-983-8904

New Brunswick, Newfoundland and Labrador, Nova Scotia, and Prince Edward Island

Maritime Centre
1505 Barrington Street, 16th Floor
Halifax, Nova Scotia B3J 3K5
Tel.: 1-877-376-9902 (toll free)
Fax: 902-426-7275

Northwest Territories and Nunavut

Canada Place Building
9700 Jasper Avenue NW, Suite 725
Edmonton, Alberta T5J 4C3
Tel.: 1-877-376-9902 (toll free)
Fax: 780-495-2466

Ontario

Federal Building — London
451 Talbot Street, Suite 303
London, Ontario N6A 5C9
Tel.: 1-877-376-9902 (toll free)
Fax: 519-645-5139

Federal Building — Hamilton
55 Bay Street N, 9th Floor
Hamilton, Ontario L8R 3P7
Tel.: 1-877-376-9902 (toll free)
Fax: 905-572-4066

Place Bell Building
160 Elgin Street, 11th Floor, Suite B-100
Ottawa, Ontario K2P 2P7
Tel.: 1-877-376-9902 (toll free)
Fax: 613-996-0949

25 St. Clair Avenue E, 6th Floor
Toronto, Ontario M4T 1M2
Tel.: 1-877-376-9902 (toll free)
Fax: 416-973-7440

Quebec

Sunlife Building
1155 Metcalfe Street, Suite 950
Montreal, Quebec H3B 2V6
Tel.: 1-877-376-9902 (toll free)
Fax: 514-283-9795

1550, D'Estimauville Avenue, Suite 702
Quebec, Quebec G1J 0C4
Tel.: 1-877-376-9902
Fax: 418-648-4120

Saskatchewan

1945 Hamilton Street, Suite 600
Regina, Saskatchewan S4P 2C7
Tel.: 1-877-376-9902 (toll free)
Fax: 306-780-6947

123 2nd Avenue S, 7th Floor
Saskatoon, Saskatchewan S7K 7E6
Tel.: 1-877-376-9902 (toll free)
Fax: 306-975-5317

Appendix 3
SUPERINTENDENT'S STANDARDS

Check www.ic.gc.ca/eic/site/bsf-osb.nsf/eng/home for updates; the Standards are updated annually. For the entirety of Directive No. 11R2 please see www.ic.gc.ca/eic/site/bsf-osb.nsf/eng/br03093.html#appA. (These links were functional at the time of printing, but could change.)

Persons	S ($)	Family Unit's Available Monthly Income ($)															
		2206	2406	2606	2806	3006	3206	3406	3606	3806	4006	4206	4406	4606	4806	5106	5606
1	2006	200	400	600	800	1000	1200	1400	1600	1800	2000	2200	2400	2600	2800	3100	3600
2	2497	0	0	0	309	509	709	909	1109	1309	1509	1709	1909	2109	2309	2609	3109
3	3070	0	0	0	0	0	0	336	536	736	936	1136	1336	1536	1736	2036	2536
4	3728	0	0	0	0	0	0	0	0	0	278	478	678	878	1078	1378	1878
5	4228	0	0	0	0	0	0	0	0	0	0	0	0	378	578	878	1378
6	4768	0	0	0	0	0	0	0	0	0	0	0	0	0	0	338	838
7+	5309	0	0	0	0	0	0	0	0	0	0	0	0	0	0	0	297

THE DOWNLOAD KIT

Please use the link information you see in the box below by entering it into your computer web browser to access and download the kit.

---

http://www.self-counsel.com/updates/bankrupt/14forms.htm

Note: The forms included in the download kit are samples. Bankruptcy is not a do-it-yourself task. The forms provided will help you prepare for and understand the process. Please consult a lawyer and/or trustee for assistance.

The download kit includes:

- Glossary of terms
- Online reference materials
- Sample bankruptcy forms:
  - Affidavit of Income and Expenses
  - Assignment for the General Benefit of Creditors
  - Statement of Affairs (Non-Business Bankruptcy)
  - Bankruptcy Order
  - Third Party Guarantee Agreement
  - Third Party Deposit Agreement
  - Notice to Bankrupt of Duties
  - Notice to Creditors of First Meeting
  - Topical Items to Review with Consumer Debtor
  - Agreement Letter
  - Proof of Claim
  - Notice of Examination before the Official Receiver
  - Examination of the Bankrupt by Official Receiver
  - Notice of Impending Automatic Discharge of First-Time Bankrupt
  - Notice of Bankruptcy and First Meeting of Creditors

- Notice to Creditors of Bankrupt's Application for Discharge
- Section 170 Report
- Notice of Opposition of Discharge of Bankrupt
- Disposition of Discharge of Bankrupt before Registrar/Judge
- Absolute Order of Discharge
- Order Subject to Condition
- Order Suspending Discharge
- Consumer Proposal
- Report of Administrator on Consumer Proposal
- Report of Administrator on Consumer Proposal and Conduct of Consumer Debtor
- Notice to Creditors of Consumer Proposal
- Notice of Meeting of Creditors to Consider Consumer Proposal
- Request for Mediation Made by Trustee
- Notice of Mediation
- Notice of Cancellation of Mediation
- Mediation Settlement Agreement
- Notice of Non-Resolution by Mediation
- Income and Expense Settlement

INDEX

A

C

F

G

I

J

L

M

N

O

P

Q

R

S

T

OTHER TITLES OF INTEREST FROM SELF-COUNSEL PRESS

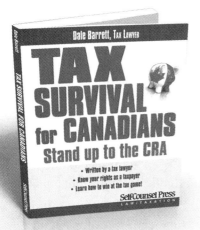

Tax Survival for Canadians: Stand Up to the CRA

Dale Barrett, Tax Lawyer
ISBN: 978-1-77040-039-9
$22.95 CAD

At any given time, there are thousands of Canadians involved in disputes with the CRA, for reasons such as owing back taxes or making an honest mistake on a tax return. Whatever the reason is for the dispute, the CRA can be an intimidating organization. If you are currently in a dispute with the CRA or fear you may become involved in one, you can remain feeling powerless or you can choose to educate yourself about the CRA, the audit process, and your rights as a taxpayer; you can gain the confidence to take a stand against the CRA!

Left unchallenged, the CRA can utilize many methods to collect including asset seizures, liens, garnishes, and court cases, which have the potential to result in prison sentences! Author and Canadian tax lawyer Dale Barrett understands how devastating those consequences can be for you and your family. He has written *Tax Survival for Canadians* to put the power back into your hands by providing you with the best strategies to deal with the CRA.

Tax Survival is the complete guide for Canadians looking to take control of their situation to reach a fair resolution with the CRA.

The Author

Dale Barrett, BCL, LLB, is an experienced Canadian tax lawyer dedicated to providing expert tax advice to hardworking Canadians who may feel powerless in resolving their tax problems. Barrett works with his clients to protect their interests and defend them against the CRA. His firm, Barrett Tax Law, specializes in assisting small-business owners and the self-employed. He lives in Toronto, Ontario and can be found at www.barretttaxlaw.com

No More Mac 'n' Cheese!

Lise Andreana

ISBN: 978-1-77040-090-0

They're the debt generation: educated, tech savvy, and often over-ambitious. Yet they're easily discouraged and distracted, and sometimes carry a sense of entitlement. Furthermore, they're smart enough to realize that they don't know everything when it comes to personal finance. No group has ever started adult life so deeply in the hole, thanks to mounting college costs, dwindling financial aid, and credit card debt.

This book covers all the important financial issues for young adults, including:

- Tips for a successful transition from the family home to first apartment

- How to maximize an employer's benefit plans

- How to set and save for future goals: vacations, wedding, cars, and deposits for a real estate purchase

The Author

As a financial advisor for the past 15 years, Lise Andreana has helped over 1,200 clients: retirees raised during the '30s and '40s, professional Boomers born during the '50s and '60s, and young professionals born to Generation X.